*Dedicated to my beloved husband Simon, the most enthusiastic
one-man cheering section imaginable.*

Contents

The Hidden Magic of Walt Disney World

TRIVIA

A Ride-by-Ride Exploration of the History, Facts, and Secrets Behind the **Magic Kingdom, Epcot, Disney's Hollywood Studios,** and **Disney's Animal Kingdom**

SUSAN VENESS
Author of the bestselling *The Hidden Magic of Walt Disney World*

A **adams**media
Avon, Massachusetts

Published by
Adams Media, a division of F+W Media, Inc.
57 Littlefield Street, Avon, MA 02322. U.S.A.
www.adamsmedia.com

ISBN 10: 1-4405-6894-4
ISBN 13: 978-1-4405-6894-7
eISBN 10: 1-4405-6895-2
eISBN 13: 978-1-4405-6895-4

Printed in the United States of America.

Printed by RR Donnelley, Harrisonburg, VA, U.S.A.
10 9 8 7 6 5 4 3
February 2015

The following are registered trademarks of The Walt Disney Company:
Adventureland, Audio-Animatronics, Disney's Animal Kingdom, Epcot,
Fantasyland, Frontierland, Indiana Jones Epic Stunt Spectacular!, Magic
Kingdom, Main Street U.S.A., Mickey Mouse, Tomorrowland, The Twilight
Zone Tower of Terror, Walt Disney World.

Many of the designations used by manufacturers and sellers to distinguish
their product are claimed as trademarks. Where those designations appear in
this book and F+W Media was aware of a trademark claim, the designations
have been printed with initial capital letters.

Cover image © iStockphoto.com.

This book is available at quantity discounts for bulk purchases.
For information, please call 1-800-289-0963.

Introduction

Are you a huge Disney World fan who knows everything there is to know about the parks? Are you planning your first trip to see The Mouse? Whether you're an Annual Passholder or are buying your first pair of mouse ears, *The Hidden Magic of Walt Disney World Trivia* gives you a chance to show what you know . . . and lets you learn something in the process! This interactive guide provides a ride-by-ride exploration of the history, magic, and fun that all four Walt Disney World parks—Magic Kingdom, Epcot, Disney's Hollywood Studios, and Disney's Animal Kingdom—have to offer. For each attraction you will find the following:

- **Trivia Questions:** one multiple-choice question and a harder fill-in-the-blank to test your park smarts
- **Fascinating Fact:** a little trivia treasure to enhance your trip or bump up your Disney IQ
- **Look For:** something special to seek out that adds extra insight to your touring

Just remember that Disney parks are dynamic, so if something has been removed, simply walk on to the next attraction or location.

In addition to the trivia, there are scavenger hunts for all four theme parks. Try them as you go from attraction to attraction or make them a tour of their own. You'll also find a Kid's

Scavenger Hunt, full of easy-to-find locations throughout the parks, and a Die-Hard Scavenger Hunt for the superfan who has been to Walt Disney World a billion times and can rattle off the entire spiel for Jungle Cruise without taking a breath. The Die-Hard Scavenger Hunt is serious bragging-rights territory, but don't be daunted if you're new to the parks. Also, since all scavenger-hunt locations are outside the attractions, you won't need to take the ride or stay for the show, which will help you avoid longer queues midday or in peak seasons.

You'll find answer keys for the trivia questions and the scavenger hunts (except the Kid's Scavenger Hunt where it's not difficult to find the items) at the back of the book, but no matter how many questions you answer or how many items you find, the most important thing is to have fun. With *The Hidden Magic of Walt Disney World Trivia*, you can keep the magic going whether you're standing in line at Space Mountain or sitting on the couch at home. It's the perfect companion for Walt Disney World fans who are between visits, in the planning stages, or in the middle of the magic.

Now . . . pick up a pencil and let's get started!

CHAPTER 1

Magic Kingdom

If you've been to the Magic Kingdom before, you know it's not unusual to see grown men cry while looking down Main Street at the castle or adults wearing those long-eared Goofy hats even if they don't have children with them. If this is your first visit, prepare to be utterly transported.

There is something undeniably magical about the Magic Kingdom. It's a sentimental blending of the intricate detail supplied by the Imagineers and an air of joyful anticipation brought by guests creating memories to last a lifetime. You know it, you love it, and now, let's see how much you know about it!

QUESTION 1

You hear the words *Walt Disney World* and your pulse quickens. It's undeniably the second "happiest place on earth"—a designation given to the Disneyland park in Anaheim, California. What was the original nickname given to Walt Disney World?

A Walt's Wonderful World of Disney

B Disneyland Florida

C Mickey's Magical Kingdom

D The Vacation Kingdom of the World

QUESTION 2

Disney loves to throw a party, especially when they can make it a yearlong celebration. What was the name given to Walt Disney World's 25th anniversary celebration?

_____

FASCINATING FACT

In 1971, when Walt Disney World's Magic Kingdom opened, seven-ride coupon books cost just $4.75. However, using the best upselling technique, more rides could be added once guests entered the park. Are you ready for an even more sobering fact? Parking was fifty cents.

LOOK FOR

Picture spots! The Kodak camera icons that were once on the park maps are no longer listed, but the picture spots remain. Here's where they're located in the Magic Kingdom, and the best way to line up your shot.

- When you first enter the park, before going under the train track, stand directly in front of the landscaping of Mickey's head, with the **train station** centered behind you.
- Stand in the fenced cutout by the rose garden (near the bridge into Tomorrowland); it's just to the left after you pass under the Plaza Rose Garden arch, with the tallest steeple of **Cinderella Castle** directly behind you.
- Stand next to the lamppost adjacent to the fenced-in geysers on the circle pathway near the exit for Big Thunder Mountain Railroad, with the mine tunnel to your left and the tallest peak of **Big Thunder Mountain** directly above you as seen through the camera. Try to time your photo so a train is whizzing by.
- Stand to the right of **Splash Mountain**, along the fence with the direction sign pointing to Splash Mountain, Liberty Square, and Adventureland to your left; the water wheel behind you; and the tallest peak of the mountain directly above you as seen through the camera.
- Stand in front of one (or more, depending on how many are in your group) of the spitting **Tiki gods**; they're located between Jungle Cruise and Magic Carpets of Aladdin.
- Pretend you're pulling the **sword from the stone**, as you face the back of Cinderella Castle. Really ham it up for the best picture.
- For another shot of **Cinderella Castle**, stand along the metal fence with the left side of the castle centered directly behind you and Sleepy Hollow refreshments to your right.

Main Street, U.S.A.

Main Street, U.S.A. is the "small-town America" we all remember but that never really existed. More idyllic than factual, Main Street tugs on your heartstrings and makes you long for a simpler, gentler time, when neighbors greeted neighbors and the smell of baking cookies filled the air.

QUESTION 1

Magic Kingdom is all about making memories, and there is one event that certainly creates special memories for very special people. What occurs on Main Street every day at 5 P.M.?

A Mickey and Minnie dance with all the couples celebrating anniversaries.

B A military veteran takes part in a flag-lowering ceremony.

C Annual Passholders are given free ice cream.

D Tinker Bell sprinkles pixie dust over the children and reminds them to follow their dreams.

QUESTION 2

Main Street is based on both Walt Disney's memories of his youth in Marceline, Missouri, and on the memories of another Imagineer who grew up in Fort Collins, Colorado. Who is this Imagineer?

Walt Disney World Railroad

Walt Disney was a visionary, and he was also a big train buff. From his earliest memories, trains were a part of his life, and his love of trains culminates in a "yesteryear experience" at each of his parks. There is a ring of authenticity about the railroad journey around the Magic Kingdom because these steam trains are, in fact, the real deal.

QUESTION I
....

Those train engines really get around! Made in the United States, they moved to Yucatán, Mexico, returned to Florida, and finally found a permanent home at Walt Disney World. How were the trains moved from their home in the Yucatán to Tampa?

A They were flown over by helicopter.

B They took the long route, over the Rocky Mountains.

C They were disassembled and shipped over.

D Their parts were boxed up and flown over on Eastern Airlines, formerly the official airline for Walt Disney World.

QUESTION 2

Which of the four Magic Kingdom trains is named for the mechanical specialist who encouraged Walt Disney's love of trains and was instrumental in getting and keeping Walt's trains on track?

FASCINATING FACT

When Walt Disney was "imagining" Disneyland, he wanted a railroad to run around the whole park. Now, every Disney resort has its railroad. For a bit of nostalgia, board at the Fantasyland station in Storybook Circus, which takes its name from the Carolwood Pacific Railroad Walt built in the backyard of his California home.

LOOK FOR

Okay, this is really cool if you're a Disney history buff. As you pass under the Main Street Train Station (which is based on a Victorian train station in Saratoga Springs, New York), head over to the stroller rental area. Along the wall, you'll find pictures of Walt Disney working on and riding the Carolwood Pacific Railroad he had built in his backyard. The delight Walt took in his little train set is obvious, and you can't help but smile along with him.

Fantasyland

From the gruesome, graphic fairy tales collected throughout Europe, to the Brothers Grimm's less explicit stories with an overt religious overtone, to the sanitized happily-ever-after of the Magic Kingdom, beloved tales come to life in the park's busy, bustling Fantasyland.

QUESTION I

Until she (and Jiminy Cricket) became a symbol of the Magic Kingdom, Tinker Bell was considered a minor character that would never have another role after the movie *Peter Pan*. Now, she's a beloved fixture for millions of fans. When did Tinker Bell begin her nightly flights over Fantasyland in Magic Kingdom?

A 1975

B 1980

C 1985

D 1990

QUESTION 2

Fantasyland underwent a major transformation in 2012, adding Belle, Ariel, and Snow White to its lineup of featured Disney characters. But there have been other new kids on the block over the past forty years. Which existing attractions in Fantasyland were there when the park opened?

Prince Charming Regal Carrousel

The Prince Charming Regal Carrousel began its career in Detroit, Michigan, in 1917, and then moved to Maplewood, New Jersey, before finding a permanent home in the Magic Kingdom. Although royal ownership of the carrousel has changed, this ride remains a favorite of young knights and ladies fair.

QUESTION I

Using the French spelling of *carousel*, the Prince Charming Regal Carrousel is, as the story goes, a training device for the prince's knights. In which skill does it train them?

A Horseback riding

B Riding in formation for parades

C Jousting

D Sword fighting in battle

QUESTION 2

All of the rows on the ride have five charging steeds, except one. Instead of horses, what is the immobile option and which two characters adorn it?

FASCINATING FACT

Before her marriage to Prince Charming, Cinderella owned the carousel. Then her prince commandeered it as a fancy version of other training equipment he has stashed away in the countryside. Guests never see the country version, but one thing is for certain: If that horse with the golden ribbon on its tail ever was Cinderella's (as popular myth contends), it certainly isn't anymore.

LOOK FOR

The letter *C* is etched on the mirrors. A convenient choice, it turns out, as it works equally well for Cinderella or for her prince, Charming. Should anyone else ever take possession of it in the future, the letter *C* can stand for Carousel.

The Many Adventures of Winnie the Pooh

Favorite scenes from the Winnie-the-Pooh tale, "The Blustery Day," are re-created here, but the real attraction is bouncing along with Tigger.

QUESTION 1

Winnie-the-Pooh and his friends from the Hundred Acre Wood are popular with the younger crowd, making wait times nearly prohibitive in peak seasons. Because of this, Disney added an interactive queue, with fun games for riders to play while they wait. Which game is not part of Pooh's lineup?

A Musical flowers and fruits

B A talking book page

C Honeybees-on-track maze

D Tigger in the Box

QUESTION 2

Pooh is a creative fellow, as evidenced by the mailbox located just outside his treehouse. What has the tubby cubby used as a mailbox flag?

_____

FASCINATING FACT

Christopher Robin, son of author A. A. Milne, really did have a pooh-bear—and a stuffed tiger, kangaroo, donkey, and piglet. Although Owl and Rabbit were added to the stories, the rest of the Hundred Acre Wood's characters were based on Christopher Robin's childhood toys. If you want to visit them, they "live" in the New York Public Library.

LOOK FOR

Just after you enter the queue, look at the enlarged Chapter 1 to your right. It shows a map of the Hundred Acre Wood, but the interesting part is the directional compass. Instead of the standard initials—N, S, E, and W—a certain bear has been honored.

Mad Tea Party

Based on the Mad Hatter's merry un-birthday party scene in Lewis Carroll's classic tale *Alice's Adventures in Wonderland*, and Disney's animated movie *Alice in Wonderland*, the Mad Tea Party is more popularly known as "the teacups" or "that spinning ride."

QUESTION I
. . . .

Called Mad Tea Party in the California and Florida parks, the attraction found its way into Disney's Hong Kong, Tokyo, and Paris parks, but by other names. Which one is not a title for this ride?

A Mad Hatter's Merry Un-Birthday Party

B Alice's Tea Party

C Mad Hatter Tea Cups

D Mad Hatter's Tea Cups

QUESTION 2

Alice's adventures sprang from the imagination of an Oxford scholar who placed great value on his privacy. Because of this, he chose to write under the nom de plume Lewis Carroll. What is the real name of this famous children's author?

_____

FASCINATING FACT

After a long, exhausting, convoluted conversation about time, the Mad Hatter in Lewis Carroll's *Alice's Adventures in Wonderland* reveals that his watch has stopped at six o'clock, which is why it is always teatime for him and his friend, the March Hare.

LOOK FOR

To the left of the topiary at the front of the attraction, you'll find a blue leaf with a quote from Randy Pausch. Why are his inspirational words included near the teacups? A professor at Carnegie Mellon University before his untimely death in 2008, Pausch founded the Alice Project, a 3-D animation software program that encourages computer science proficiency in high school and college students. The project is titled after Lewis Carroll's *Alice's Adventures in Wonderland*. Disney's publishing company, Hyperion, also published Pausch's now-famous *The Last Lecture*.

Enchanted Tales with Belle

How did you get so lucky to be here on the night when Belle and the Beast fall in love? No matter, it *is* that very night. You get a sneak peek at Belle's pre-dinner preparations, and an enchanting, interactive retelling of the story, possibly with you in it.

QUESTION I

The outside of Maurice's cottage reflects his personality to a tee. The roof sags a bit; one of the two mismatched chimneys is held up by a wooden plank; the fence is rough and mended with cast-offs. But there is one feminine touch. What is it?

A Sweetheart roses adorn the garden trellises.

B The shutters have heart-shaped cutouts.

C There are big pots of flowers nestled in the landscaping.

D An impromptu tea party has been set up in the backyard.

QUESTION 2

Belle and the Beast's friends all feature in their story, and volunteers from the audience are encouraged to play roles doled out by the exuberant Wardrobe and an enthusiastic Cast Member. When it comes time for someone to be chosen to portray the Wardrobe, what does she say?

FASCINATING FACT

There are varying degrees of sophistication here, from the state-of-the-art Audio-Animatronics of the Wardrobe, to simpler (though even more dramatic) technology for Lumiere, to the simplest of props used in the interactive storytelling segment. The magical mirror is mesmerizing, as are Lumiere's movements, and while you cannot see how the mirror's magical portal effect is done, you can easily see how Lumiere comes to life. If knowing how the magic works makes it more magical for you, linger in the library for a few moments after the show ends, but remember to keep it magical by not telling anyone if you choose to discover the secret.

LOOK FOR

You could spend an hour just looking at the details along the queue (and you might, if you visit in peak season), which is filled with bits and pieces of items Maurice has repurposed. But don't miss something he made specifically for its pretty charm. Notice that the sign displaying the wait time for Enchanted Tales with Belle is a miniature version of Maurice's cottage. Cute, isn't it?

Under the Sea ~ Journey of the Little Mermaid

Maybe it really is better down where it's wetter, if Under the Sea ~ Journey of the Little Mermaid is anything to go by. It is delightful storytelling with that classic Disney touch, bringing the familiar tale to its rightful place in Fantasyland.

QUESTION 1

Scuttle isn't the most accurate interpreter of the "human stuff" Ariel presents to him for clarification. In Scuttle-speak, what is Ariel using as she swims above you in the first scene after you travel under the sea?

A A whatsit

B A thingamabob

C A dinglehopper

D A snarfblat

QUESTION 2

Lower the "sandbar" on your clamshell and head underwater, where a hot crustacean band is playing, Sebastian is singing his heart out, and sea slugs and turtles are cutting a rug. What is the octopus doing in this colorful, musical scene?

FASCINATING FACT

Oh no! What's happened to the Little Mermaid? Everything seemed to be going so well for her, but now Ariel has become the masthead on the front half of a wrecked ship! What could be the explanation for this odd placement? Every Cast Members surveyed gave the same answer you probably came up with: "I have no idea." Let's just say it makes an impressive, if baffling, entry to a charming attraction.

Seven Dwarfs Mine Train

They're dig-dig-digging the whole day through, and now you get to join the Seven Dwarfs as they mine for gems, before taking a high-speed twisting, turning, swinging ride home, "hi-hoing" all the way.

QUESTION 1

Snow White and the Seven Dwarfs isn't a new theme for Disney. From the animated movie to theme park attractions in Disney parks worldwide, it's a classic tale in every sense of the word. But there is something that makes Seven Dwarfs Mine Train different from all the rest. What is it?

A The evil witch never shows up.

B It's told from the dwarfs' point of view.

C Snow White is now a queen.

D Sleepy has changed his name to Peppy.

QUESTION 2

As you make your way through the Seven Dwarfs' stomping grounds, you'll notice this is a coaster like no other. In fact, Disney patented the design. What part of the ride vehicle design has never been done with a coaster before?

FASCINATING FACT

When imagining a big new Fantasyland expansion, original blueprints called for a princess meet-and-greet location on the grounds where Seven Dwarfs Mine Train now sits. Leaked concept art generated guest feedback against the girly-land feel of the original plans, so Imagineers rummaged through shelved ideas and found a longed-for coaster experience to take its place.

LOOK FOR

Disney Imagineers are masters of the smooth transition, making buildings do double duty when it's necessary for them to blend with more than one area. Here at Seven Dwarfs, the front of the mountain is forest, blending with the older portion of Fantasyland and Maurice's cottage next door. At the back, the scene turns seaside, a harmonious theme compatible with the nearby Journey of the Little Mermaid.

Mickey's PhilharMagic

Donald is always causing trouble. In spite of Mickey's admonition not to touch the magician's hat, Donald can't resist. Even a simple thing like leading an orchestra goes disastrously wrong, until Mickey returns to save the day.

QUESTION 1

Donald is not very good at making merry melodies, but one instrument doesn't appear to need a conductor. What tune is the cheerful piccolo playing when Donald decides to show the orchestra who is boss?

A The theme song from the Mickey Mouse Club

B "When You Wish upon a Star"

C "The Sorcerer's Apprentice" from *Fantasia*

D "Zip-A-Dee-Doo-Dah"

QUESTION 2

If you've been to a Disney park before, you know the drill: stand back, because the doors leading to the show area will open toward you. What fun twist does stage manager Goofy give to the doors at *Mickey's PhilharMagic*?

FASCINATING FACT

Donald and Mickey aren't the only ones performing at Fantasyland's concert hall. Check out some of the other surprising entertainers whose concert posters line the walls before you reach the lobby. Genie, being blue, sings the blues; Ariel has a choral group (get it? Like, coral . . . ?); and you are cordially invited to spend an evening with Wheezy of *Toy Story* fame.

LOOK FOR

Browse the gift shop at the end of the show, or take a quick glance as you walk back into Fantasyland. See those musical stands on the shelves along the ceiling? Most of them are shaped a lot like Mickey's head.

Peter Pan's Flight

You can fly, you can fly, you can fly! When asked for their feedback on the concept for a Pooh attraction, youngsters said their greatest desire was to bounce with Tigger. The enduring popularity of Peter Pan's Flight proves they also love to fly with Pan. The ride is so popular that if you line up after 10 A.M., you may be tempted to rephrase it—"you can stand, you can stand, you can stand."

QUESTION I

Flying over London at night is one of the attraction's most memorable scenes. Which London icons can you see from your ship?

A Tower Bridge and Houses of Parliament

B Big Ben clock tower and the London Eye

C Saint Paul's Cathedral and Houses of Parliament

D Tower Bridge and Big Ben clock tower

QUESTION 2

As you fly through the window into the Darling children's nursery, Wendy is reading a story to John and Michael. How can you tell Peter Pan is nearby?

FASCINATING FACT

At one time the front section of Tinker Bell's Treasures—now Fantasy Faire—was modeled after the Darling children's nursery, while the back section was Captain Hook's pirate ship. A tragic loss, indeed.

LOOK FOR

In the scene where Pan and Captain Hook are fighting on the mast of the ship, Hook is leading with his hooked left hand, the sword in his right hand raised above and behind his head. What's up with that awkward position? In the Disneyland version of the ride, Hook's hook has mysteriously traveled to his right hand (oops!), in spite of the movie having established a left-hand hook. Orlando got it right, but Disneyland Paris defaulted back to the right-hand hook. Perhaps the ineffective technique of the captain leading with his hook in Orlando is a wink toward this curious error.

"it's a small world"

Say what you will about the song, the attraction is a classic, and for good reason. It's a hopeful testament to a joyful future, where differences coexist peacefully with common ground. You can even brighten a child's day when you wave at him or her though the windows as he or she is having lunch in Pinocchio Village Haus.

QUESTION 1

By the time your journey past happy, singing dolls ends, you'll have that infernal song stuck in your head for the rest of the day. As catchy as it is, the song we know now wasn't the Sherman Brothers' original proposal. What did Richard and Robert Sherman have in mind for the attraction's song before it became "a small world after all"?

A A blending of several national anthems

B A triumphant marching tune

C A symphony similar to "Brahms's Lullaby"

D A children's chorus singing popular childhood songs

QUESTION 2

It's obvious now which movies inspired attractions, but Imagineers have often pulled ideas from Disney films and movie shorts. Which 1945 Disney animated film included a "La Piñata" scene that inspired the look of the children in "it's a small world"?

FASCINATING FACT

Not only is the attraction a charming and uplifting experience, there is something along the queue that has serious "feel-good" appeal. Guests can't resist throwing coins into the water along the walkway, and Disney can't resist putting it to good use. So toss your coins in and make a wish. The money is donated to Give Kids the World, an organization that makes wishes come true for children with life-threatening illnesses. Feel good, knowing you've helped Give Kids the World bring deserving children to Walt Disney World.

LOOK FOR

Check out that wacky duo—the delusional Don Quixote and his sidekick, Sancho Panza. Don and San are clearly off on another adventure in chivalry (or insanity), and you can find them on the left-hand side of the ride just as you enter the Spain section. See them riding their mighty wooden steeds? Don is the one in front, holding the sword.

Liberty Square

Walt Disney's patriotism is captured beautifully in Liberty Square, from the inspiring founding of our nation told at the Hall of Presidents to the replica of the Liberty Bell and the heaping plates of American comfort food served at Liberty Tree Tavern.

QUESTION 1

There is a courtyard just to the right as you face the Liberty Oak Tree, with flags honoring the United States' thirteen original colonies. Which of these states is not included?

A Georgia

B South Carolina

C Rhode Island

D Maine

QUESTION 2

We know it as the Liberty Bell, but the bell actually had five other nicknames during its early life. Can you name one of those five? Two? Three? Four? Surely not all five! Or can you?

FASCINATING FACT

The art of silhouette cutting, practiced here in Liberty Square, became wildly popular in France in the 1700s as a fanciful pastime for aristocrats, who would have their likenesses cut into black paper. France's finance minister under Louis XV, Étienne de Silhouette, who was notorious for starving the good citizens of France through unfeasible taxation, was a big fan of this paper art. Thus, the citizens dubbed these frivolities "Silhouettes."

LOOK FOR

Tourists with their heads and arms sticking through the large pillory have found their way into photo albums all over the world. But take a look at the tiny stocks to the left of the large version. No, it's not a punishment tool for naughty colonial dogs and cats; it's a hand-and-ankle stocks. The stocks are a fun photo op here, but they were brutal forms of torture in their day.

The Hall of Presidents

The history of the United States was shaped, in part, by the people who have led this great country. The Hall of Presidents focuses on some of the most charismatic of these men, and the decisions they made that changed the nation . . . and the world.

QUESTION 1
. . . .

As the roll is called, each president in turn silently makes a small gesture of acknowledgement. Which president, besides Presidents Lincoln and Washington, is the first one to offer a speech?

A Ronald Reagan

B Jimmy Carter

C Bill Clinton

D Barack Obama

QUESTION 2

The incomparable Disney legend Blaine Gibson sculpted the busts of every president except one. Gibson's apprentice sculpted President Obama, as well as Barbossa and Jack Sparrow in the Pirates of the Caribbean attraction. What is this apprentice's name?

FASCINATING FACT

As a young boy, Walt Disney greatly admired President Lincoln, so it was a natural that he would want this historical figure included in the 1964 World's Fair and in his theme parks. To ensure the highest degree of accuracy, Disney's version of President Lincoln's face was taken from a copy of a life mask (a casting of the president's face while he was still alive) created by sculptor Leonard Volk in 1860.

Haunted Mansion

The Haunted Mansion is classic Disney storytelling at its best, told through layers of detail and numerous subplots. Discover secrets of the ghostly bride, attend a séance and a swinging wake, and maybe even take an unexpected hitchhiker home with you.

QUESTION 1
....

What are the names of the three hitchhiking ghosts at the Haunted Mansion?

A Wathel, Claude, and Xavier

B Bud, Randolph, and Jonas

C Ezra, Gus, and Phineas

D Casper, Marley, and Sir Spooksalot

QUESTION 2

Some of the characters that you see in the graveyard section of the queue are familiar friends from the attraction inside, and some are new additions. But one new character was actually part of the original concept. He didn't end up in the final story, but he's memorialized on Ravenscroft's crypt. Who is he?

FASCINATING FACT

You may have noticed the "chicken exit," off the right-hand side of the queue just after you exit the stretch room. But there's another hallway that holds a couple of special props that most guests will never see unless they're dignitaries or VIPs. There, you'll find a series of bells that, in a proper working mansion, would be used by the residents to contact the servants. Here, they're Imagineer signatures; each bell is labeled in honor of the key Imagineers who worked on the Haunted Mansion. Honored are Yale Gracey, Claude Coats, Mark Davis, Xavier Atencio, Leota Toombs, and a certain Grandfather McKim, whose bell remembers Sam McKim, the Imagineer who created the original concept drawings for the Haunted Mansion.

LOOK FOR

The ballroom scene is probably the most famous scene in the whole attraction, and the level of detail is enormous. From the dueling paintings to the waltzing ghosts, it's hard to absorb it all as you pass by. But take a look at the birthday cake on the far-right end of the dining room table; appropriately enough, it has thirteen candles.

Liberty Square Riverboat

Ah, the lazy days of summer. It doesn't get much more relaxing than this, and even though you're traveling a long, long way (from colonial New England to the barren Southwest to the shores of New York's Hudson River Valley), your riverboat journey is so delightful it feels like only minutes.

QUESTION 1

The Mississippi River of Mark Twain's time certainly saw its share of paddleboats, and that bygone era is recreated in Liberty Square. However, the waterway the *Liberty Belle* sails on has another name. What is it?

A Mighty Miss

B Rivers of America

C Worldwide Waterways

D The Happiest River on Earth

QUESTION 2

As you begin your journey, you discover that Samuel Clemens, riverboat pilot turned author and humorist, has joined you for your adventure. Sam provides historical snippets about the locations you're passing, but he also gives safety warnings, one of which involves not sitting on the boat's railings. What is the reason he gives for avoiding this behavior?

FASCINATING FACT

Shortly before you return to the boat dock, your ship passes a certain haunted mansion. You've heard the story about a ghostly bride leading men to their doom, but Sam Clemens offers another reason for the ghoulish goings-on. The story he heard is that the mansion was built on sacred Indian burial grounds, a theory supported by the Indian village you just passed. However, he, like the 999 inhabitants of the house in question, thinks it's just a tall tale. Or is it?

LOOK FOR

This one is a "Listen For" because it's just a fun little tidbit. Listen for the leadsman, who is singing out the water depths as you enjoy a relaxing excursion. His job is to warn the pilot if the water level is too low to cross safely. What is the lowest safe level? Two fathoms, which equals twelve feet. What does the leadsman do when the water is two fathoms? He sings out, "Mark twain," as in, "I have marked this area at a safe two fathoms."

Frontierland

The time frame in Frontierland spans 1770–1880, which you'll see in the clapboard houses of 1840s Saint Louis, to the rustic log buildings of the Wild West, to the WestMex style of Pecos Bill Tall Tale Inn and Cafe. Mock gunfights erupt without warning, singing cowboys make the occasional appearance, and stuffed animal heads can't resist joining in the fun.

QUESTION I

It wouldn't be the wild, wild West without the chance to shoot at unsuspecting targets. Although Frontierland Shootin' Arcade no longer uses lead bullets, opting for a beam of safe infrared light, the skill level is roughly the same (minimal). Which of the following is not a target in the Boot Hill diorama?

A A shovel digging a grave

B A steam train

C A canteen

D A caravan of covered wagons

QUESTION 2

Which existing attractions in Frontierland were there on opening day?

Country Bear Jamboree

Git yer yee-haw on. The country bears are havin' a jamboree! It's good ole-fashioned slapstick, with a grizzly twist.

QUESTION I

As Gomer plays an introduction on the piano in the opening scene, there are several large advertisements on the wall to his left. One of the ads is for the dental services of Dr. Winch, who specializes in dentures for bears. Which feature of his dentures does Dr. Winch promote?

A They "Make Having Dentures Bear-able."

B They "Won't Get All Furry"

C They "Taste Like a Pine Tree on a Summer Day."

D They have "Built-In Grizzly Grip."

QUESTION 2

Big Al is arguably Country Bear Jamboree's most popular character. Which Imagineer is he based on?

FASCINATING FACT

Big Al's rendition of "Blood on the Saddle" is one of the most memorable songs in the show, but Al never reveals what happened to cause the bleeding. Country singer Tex Ritter performed the tune (as the voice of Big Al), and while only the chorus is included in Country Bear Jamboree, the original has two more verses. Apparently the cowboy won't be riding broncos anymore, since one of them fell on him and smashed his head in. Probably best left unsaid, hey?

LOOK FOR

Masks representing Comedy and Tragedy are icons of the theater, and the bears haven't left this important detail out at Country Bear Jamboree. But here they take a slightly different, if appropriate, twist. Take a look at the masks as you enter or exit the theater; instead of human faces, they're bears.

Splash Mountain

Splash Mountain is based on the classic story *Song of the South*, originally released in 1946 and deemed too controversial to be rereleased in its entirety for home viewing. This sail along a Georgia river tells the tales of Br'er Rabbit, Br'er Bear, and Br'er Fox, who are constantly makin' mischief.

QUESTION 1

Most attraction concepts have a "working title," which may or may not change when the attraction debuts. For example, Monsters Inc. Laugh Floor was Laugh Floor Comedy Club before it opened, Great Moments from the Movies became the Great Movie Ride, and the original idea that became "it's a small world" went by the working title Children of the World. What was the working title for Splash Mountain?

A Br'er Rabbit's Laughing Place

B Zip-a-Dee-Doo-Drop

C Briar Patch Br'ers

D Splash Mountain

QUESTION 2

Br'er Fox and Br'er Bear aren't having much luck capturing Br'er Rabbit, but when they finally do, it's in a rather ingenious way. What do they trap him in?

FASCINATING FACT

Song of the South, the movie featuring animated scenes on which the attraction is based, began as a collection of writings by Joel Chandler Harris that documented stories told to him by slaves on Georgia's Turnwold Plantation. His first collection of tales was *Uncle Remus: His Songs and Sayings: The Folklore of the Old Plantation*. Harris created Uncle Remus (based on Uncle George of Turnwold) to be a character who occasionally "visited" him during his workdays at the *Atlanta Constitution* newspaper.

LOOK FOR

The small wooden door and log mailbox on the front of Briar Patch leads to Br'er Rabbit's house. He's the only one who can use them, of course, but if you go inside the Briar Patch shop, you'll see his home set up along the ceiling.

Big Thunder Mountain Railroad

You'll get to work in the mining mayhem at Big Thunder Mountain, checking on the miner's progress through special subterranean periscopes, or testing air quality and pumping air into the shafts so the workers can breathe safely. You can even help create a new tunnel. But watch out; you may find that this work is a blast!

QUESTION I

Which company is still supplying explosives to Big Thunder Mining Company, even after the mine had a big update in 2012?

A Lytum and Hyde

B Duk and Cuver

C Acme Dynamite Inc.

D Explosives R Us

QUESTION 2
....
Big Thunder Mining Company's pay scale is meant to be seen only by the paymaster, but you won't have any trouble seeing it. The foreman is at the top of the pay scale with $10.48 per day, but the lowly mucker is at the bottom of the totem pole, having a horrible job with very little reward. How much does the mucker make each day?

FASCINATING FACT
See that crate next to the drinking fountain in front of Big Thunder Mountain? It's meant to be shipped to Fire Chief W. Ray Colburn. Chief Colburn was the real fire chief of the Reedy Creek Fire Department, controlled by Disney, and you'll find another reference to him on a barrel over by Peter Pan's Flight.

LOOK FOR
As you walk through the queue, look at some of the junk collecting in the rafters. It really is no wonder there's trouble in the mine when you consider how much dynamite, gunpowder, and open-flame lanterns are scattered around.

Tom Sawyer Island

Considered a minor attraction by those who have not made the short raft ride to this little plot of land, Tom Sawyer Island is beloved by those who have discovered the benefit of letting overstimulated youngsters loose in a playground straight out of any child's most vivid imagination.

QUESTION 1

While exploring the mines and caves, you come upon several interesting features. But you won't find one of the following during your underground explorations. Which one is it?

A A formation that looks like two ghostly eyes and a mouth

B Veins and chunks of gold

C Injun Joe's skeleton

D Water that appears to run uphill

QUESTION 2

You know it as Fort Langhorn, a military outpost on the farthest reaches of town. But as you journey by river, Sam Clemens tells you the fort is posing as something far more benign. What does he say it claims to be?

_____

FASCINATING FACT

How do you create a Midwestern feel on an island in subtropical Florida? By using "look-alike" plants. Some of the plants on the island are native to the Mississippi River and are able to thrive in Orlando, but many temperate-climate plants would not survive the heat and rain of a Florida summer. In these cases, local plants with a similar look, or plants that can be trimmed to look like the real thing, are substituted. You'll find this adaptation all over Walt Disney World.

LOOK FOR

As you wander the island, look at the dock across the river in front of Big Thunder Mountain. Apparently it's the launching point for freight and all-day sightseeing tours. Notice the name of the proprietor. It's Mike Fink, whose keelboats once plied these very waters hereabout but have been out of the sightseeing business since 2001.

Adventureland

Big-eyed torchbearers kneeling to the Tiki gods, jumping taran-tulas, mermaids waiting to drown you in the ocean's depths—it must be Adventureland! No self-respecting theme park would be complete without a hint of danger lurking around the corner.

QUESTION 1

There sure are a lot of woven rugs hanging around Adventure-land, and it appears they may have been made locally. What evidence of a small textile industry can be found above Island Supply?

A There are weaving looms on the roof.

B Skeins of colored yarn have been put out to dry.

C A billboard reads Handwoven Rugs for Sale.

D The shopkeeper's daughter can be seen sewing tassels on the corners of small rugs.

QUESTION 2

Pirates from the Caribbean have taken over Adventureland! They have even commandeered businesses once owned by well-established merchants. What is the name of the proprietor who has taken over El Pirata Y el Perico and renamed it Tor-tuga Tavern?

Pirates of the Caribbean

This is the "attraction that almost wasn't." Initially, Disney felt the popular Pirates of the Caribbean attraction in Disneyland would be too ho-hum for Florida, since the Caribbean was just a short cruise off the southern tip of the state. But guests had other ideas and complained . . . loudly. Aren't you glad they did?

QUESTION I

What are the two attributes the auctioneer mentions while selling off the "winsome wench"?

A She is "clean and infection-free."

B She is "stouthearted and corn fed."

C She has a "formidable superstructure and a noble lar-board side."

D She is "quick with a pint and never spills a drop."

QUESTION 2

What is the name of the pirate ship manned by Captain Barbossa in the cannon fight scene between the ship and the fort?

FASCINATING FACT

Just like Captain Jack Sparrow in the blockbuster *Pirates of the Caribbean* movie series, the attraction's Jack is found near the action but not in it. Not only is this behavior in keeping with his onscreen persona, it allowed for a smooth transition incorporating the movie character into a beloved classic attraction.

LOOK FOR

Mermaids! The first scene could account for the shipwreck you see in the second scene. Evil mermaids are swimming right next to your boat, attempting to sing you to your doom. But one of them hasn't fared well. You can see her skeleton on the sandy beach to your left. What's the song they're singing? It's "My Jolly Sailor Bold," from the fourth *Pirates of the Caribbean* movie, *On Stranger Tides*.

Jungle Cruise

No need for vaccinations or traveler's-tummy medications on this journey through exotic lands. If you can look past the groan-inducing banter (or take part in it), your jungle cruise offers whimsical highlights you'll never see along the Amazon, Nile, Congo, and Mekong Rivers.

QUESTION 1

As you reach Schweitzer Falls, your skipper is having problems steering the boat. What does the skipper ask you to do as the danger of crashing through the wall of water looms large?

A Lean!

B Move to right side of the boat!

C Jump overboard!

D Put on your Mickey ponchos!

QUESTION 2

Although Walt's vision for live animals along the Jungle Cruise never materialized, some of the animal scenes in the attraction were inspired by a Walt Disney film series. Which series was it?

_____

FASCINATING FACT

When the attraction opened, children were not only allowed to drive the boat, they were allowed to shoot the skipper's rifle when it appeared a hippo was about to attack. For a while, captains still gave a warning shot at the hippos, but in an effort to remain politically correct, fake rifles were removed from the storyline and are now only sold in Disney gift shops.

LOOK FOR

If you're a longtime Disney fan, this might upset you. But take it in the spirit of historical gems hidden within the park, and try not to be too sad. If you look at some of the tags in the wire cage just after you enter the queue, you'll see references to the much-missed Adventurer's Club nightclub, formerly on Pleasure Island. If you've never been to the Adventurers Club, it may be a blessing. In this instance, the concept of "it's better to have loved and lost than never to have loved at all" just doesn't work. Many Kungalooshing club members are still silently grieving.

Walt Disney's Enchanted Tiki Room

Birds from Germany, Ireland, Mexico, and France have migrated to Florida and still have the energy to put on a rousing show for the tourists. This is classic Disney-of-old territory, and while its theme song may be a bit catchy, the Tiki Room's stars hold the honored distinction of being Disney's first successful attempt at an Audio-Animatronics show.

QUESTION 1

Join your bird hosts José, Fritz, Pierre, and Michael in the Tiki, Tiki, Tiki, Tiki, Tiki Room. If they weren't in the show, where does José say they would be?

A They would be sitting on a pirate's shoulder.

B They would be unemployed.

C They would be in line for a Dole Whip.

D They would be in the audience.

QUESTION 2

At the end of the show, those birds really want you to get out! They have swiped a tune from the Seven Dwarfs, with a few lyrical changes. While they're hi-hoing, what is the first thing they say you should be doing?

_____

FASCINATING FACT

In the days when visitors still wore suits and dresses to theme parks, Walt Disney's Enchanted Tiki Room in Disneyland was run with a room full of enormous computers. This state-of-the-art Audio-Animatronics technology held visitors absolutely spellbound, unsure if the birds were real or Imagineered.

LOOK FOR

Even the building looks angry as the gods are awakened by the riotous singing. As you cross the bridge to enter the attraction, look at the small thatched dome, just to the left of the Tiki Room sign on the roof. Those are some angry eyes up there!

The Magic Carpets of Aladdin

Although they are nowhere to be seen, Aladdin and Jasmine are with you in spirit as you fly over Agrabah on your own magic carpet.

QUESTION 1

Jasmine surely wouldn't allow this character to be left out! Whose likeness can be seen on the front and back sections of the flying carpet?

A Iago

B Jafar

C Rajah

D The Sultan

QUESTION 2

The tower holding Genie's lamp features Genie and Abu, Aladdin's monkey, but there is one more creature depicted below the lamp. What is it?

Swiss Family Treehouse

Every kid dreams of having a treehouse, especially if it has all the comforts of home like the one the Swiss Family Robinson inhabits. Be sure to listen for the organ playing in the living room.

QUESTION I

This tree isn't exactly natural, but there is something striking about it that wasn't created by Imagineers. What is it?

A It has holes bored by woodpeckers.

B There is a real beehive in the upper branches.

C It's covered in Spanish moss.

D Stray arrows from cowboy and Indian fights in Frontierland frequently embed themselves in the bark.

QUESTION 2

The Robinsons are a creative family. What they couldn't salvage from the shipwreck, they made from found items. In this case, they did a little of both. The sink in the living room was made from two items. What are they?

FASCINATING FACT

Originally all of the plants surrounding the Swiss Family Treehouse were plants the family could use, such as papyrus, rubber, medicinal plants, and food-producing plants. Oddly enough, although the family had plenty to eat in the produce department, there aren't any fish in the rivers that surround them.

LOOK FOR

When you reach the top of the tree, reward yourself with a look around. You'll get some interesting views of the waters around the treehouse and the nearby Jungle Cruise.

Tomorrowland

You haven't left Earth, but you've entered a city of the future when humans, aliens, and robots live and work in harmony, their lives enhanced by technology. All around you'll see the everyday trapping of life—communications centers, transportation ports, entertainment venues, and even a prison. Oh, and an oddly placed carousel from the past, a quaint reminder of what progress looked like in the twentieth century.

QUESTION 1

Tomorrowland is a thriving hub of activity, a futuristic city center. Which of the following businesses is not located in Tomorrowland?

A Star Command Headquarters

B Cosmic Transgalactic Co.

C Galactic Federation Prisoner Teleport Center

D Rockettower Plaza Station

QUESTION 2

Two science-fiction films from the 1930s inspired the updated 1994 version of Tomorrowland. What are the names of the two movies?

_____

FASCINATING FACT

Even aliens drink Coke. Check out the boxes outside the Cool Ship drink kiosk. They fit the Tomorrowland theme well, but they're really a three-dimensional advertising for Coca-Cola. Notice the crates are filled with an Earth Export containing high levels of taste, and the bar code isn't really a bar code. It's an "Enjoy Ice Code" code. Clever.

LOOK FOR

Several spaceships have landed in Tomorrowland, but two of them are striking examples of our past and present perceptions of what a space vehicle might look like. The spaceship on top of the Disney Vacation Club kiosk is straight out of the B-movies of the 1930s and 1940s. The red Thirst Rangers ship is sleeker, more modern, and ever-so-slightly reminiscent of Stitch's space cruiser, though it is not meant to be Stitch's ship.

Monsters, Inc. Laugh Floor

If you're a monster, is it more fun to garner screams or laughs? Monsters, Inc. Laugh Floor makes the argument that laughs generate more energy, as it pokes gentle fun at audience members and cracks corny jokes. But some of the best material comes from the crowd, especially when it's contributed by a child or a reluctant volunteer.

QUESTION I

The opening jokes are a bit groan-inducing, prompting Roz to issue a warning. What terrifying consequence does she say will result if you don't laugh enough during the show?

A A monster will follow you home.

B Sully will be lurking under your bed tonight.

C You'll make Mike cry.

D There might not be enough power to open the exit doors.

QUESTION 2
....

To keep the laughs coming show after show, guests are invited to text their own jokes to the Laugh Floor using a special number and a keyword. What is the keyword?

_____

FASCINATING FACT

Everyone loves "That Guy." He probably didn't want to be here in the first place, which is exactly why he was chosen as the "victim," but generally That Guy turns into a good sport for the sake of the show. If you don't want to be That Guy, sit toward the front or way in back. If you do want to be That Guy, look a bit put-out and sit toward the center of your section.

LOOK FOR

Humorous notices have been pinned to the bulletin board, so check them out as you wait for the show doors to open. There appears to be an eye missing, and some lucky monster has won the Bed Wetter Award.

Buzz Lightyear's Space Ranger Spin

Evil Emperor Zurg's robotic army is trying to steal all the Crystallic Fusion Power Cells. Only Buzz Lightyear and his new recruits (you) can save the planet from powerlessness.

QUESTION 1

Andy certainly has a vivid imagination. Just as he did at Toy Story Midway Mania! at Disney's Hollywood Studios park, Andy has incorporated many of his toys into his make-believe world with Buzz Lightyear. In this attraction, which childhood toy is not represented by a similar galactic version?

A Jack in the Box

B Rock 'Em Sock 'Em Robots

C A marionette

D An Atomic Disintegrator ray gun

QUESTION 2

How many megavolts does each C Cell battery at the entry to the attraction contain?

FASCINATING FACT

If you listen closely during the short section just after the first main room, you might hear Zurg say, "Guards, seize them . . . and their little green friends, too!" It's a fun twist on the Wicked Witch's famous line in the childhood classic, *The Wizard of Oz*.

Walt Disney's Carousel of Progress

Walt Disney's Carousel of Progress began its life at the 1964 World's Fair in New York and then moved to Disneyland in California before making its permanent home in Orlando's Magic Kingdom. This propensity for change is reflected in the attraction, but not just because it's *about* change and progress. The family's home does some pretty wacky remodeling, too.

QUESTION I

Not only do the decades fly by as you spin through the twentieth century's progress, so do the holidays. Each time you move to a new scene, your host, John, mentions today's celebration. Which holiday is not included in Carousel of Progress?

A Halloween

B Valentine's Day

C Thanksgiving

D Fourth of July

QUESTION 2

John, his wife, Sarah, their daughter, Patty, and rascally Uncle Orville call each other by name several times during the show. But what is the name of John and Sarah's son?

FASCINATING FACT

When the Carousel Theater of Progress opened at the 1964 World's Fair, the time frame was much more convincing. Scene One took place just before the turn of the century; Scene Two showcased inventions of the 1920s; Scene Three featured the dawn of electricity in the 1940s; and Scene Four depicted the modern-day 1960s. This final scene has been updated five times to keep up with the theme of progress. Although Disney indicates the family spans four generations over one hundred years, it's curious that each generation has exactly the same familial makeup with the same names and the same faces. Oops!

LOOK FOR

It's clear from John's descriptions of the events of the day that time is passing rapidly, but watch what happens outside his windows and what becomes of the rooms on either side of the kitchen. The view from the left-hand window begins with a rural home down the street, becomes a hardware store in town, reverts to woodland, and ends with a view of a tree and a fence. All of the rooms on the left side change, and only the second room you see on the right—Patricia's bedroom—stays the same until the final scene.

Tomorrowland Transit Authority PeopleMover

There are no frills here, no thrills, nothing overly high-tech by today's standards, and yet, the Tomorrowland Transit Authority PeopleMover remains a fan favorite that easily stands the test of time.

QUESTION I

You may have known it as the WEDWay, or perhaps as the TTA. It's real name is the Tomorrowland Transit Authority People-Mover, but as you're traveling around the "city of tomorrow," your narrator mentions yet another name. What is it?

A Rockettower Rover

B Highway in the Sky

C Spaceport Speeder

D Cosmic Commuter

QUESTION 2

In its original incarnation, the TTA's spiel included a shout-out to Mr. Tom Morrow, whose friends from Saturn had arrived. The reference to Tom Morrow was removed during a refurbishment but reinstated in 2010. Who is Tom Morrow now supposed to contact about flight arrangements?

FASCINATING FACT

The Tomorrowland Transit Authority has its origins in the 1964 World's Fair exhibit, Magic Skyway, sponsored by Ford Motor Company. WED Enterprises (Disney) created the propulsion system that moved Ford convertibles (minus their engines) along a track. This technology was then used in Disneyland's WEDWay PeopleMover, which was re-created in Walt Disney World in 1975.

LOOK FOR

When you enter the first tunnel, look at the top of the windows to your left if you're facing forward, or to your right if you're facing backward. You'll see words reflected on the windows, which read, "City of Tomorrow is a great electric machine working for you!" In a strange, future-speak way, it is referring to the City of Tomorrow display you will see.

Astro Orbiter

Jump into your Buck Rogers–style rocket ship and head into space . . . at least, the space surrounding the attraction. At one time, the tower supporting the rocket ships was a mockup of a *Saturn V* launch vehicle, having evolved from Disneyland's basic Dumbo-style ride but with rocket-shaped vehicles.

QUESTION 1

During a 1994 remodel, Magic Kingdom's original Star Jets changed shape. They are definitely rockets now, but what did they look like when the attraction first opened?

A They looked like space shuttles.

B They looked like fat cucumbers.

C They looked like flying saucers.

D They looked like blimps with tailfins.

QUESTION 2

Astro Orbiters have only had two names at Walt Disney World, but their ancestors in Disneyland had four. Starting with the 1956 original, what are the first three names the Disneyland's Astro Orbiters attraction had?

FASCINATING FACT

Rocket Jets included signage that was appropriate to the times, which indicated that gentlemen should enter the ride vehicle first and sit in the back. Then ladies should take the center seat, and children should sit in the front. As social sensibilities changed, so did the signage, which evolved to indicate that the tallest passenger should sit in the back. We were funny way back then, weren't we?

LOOK FOR

As you ride the Astro Orbiters, you'll either be looking at the view over Tomorrowland or you'll have your eyes closed. At least open them long enough to check out Jupiter as you fly by and see if you can locate the Big Red Spot.

Space Mountain

In reality, Space Mountain is not much more dynamic than Big Thunder Mountain Railroad, but the black abyss of outer space makes this attraction seem much, much wilder!

QUESTION 1

As you make your way toward the launch pad for your journey into outer space, you'll notice a few references to Starport Seventy-Five. Why has Tomorrowland's space port been given the designation *seventy-five*?

A That's how old the lead Imagineer was when he designed the attraction.

B That's how many prototypes were used in designing the ride vehicle.

C That's the number of Imagineers who worked on the project.

D Space Mountain opened in 1975.

QUESTION 2

Remember, you're in a city of the future, with the infrastructure (like electricity) that is apparently still necessary even when transportation no longer runs on fossil fuels and teleporting is a reality. What is the tag line for Tomorrowland Light & Power Company, attached to Starport Seventy-Five?

FASCINATING FACT

A version of Space Mountain was originally imagined for Disneyland in the mid-1960s, but the technology needed to create and run the ride was not yet available. When the Magic Kingdom opened in 1971, guests were eager for a true thrill ride—meaning, a roller coaster—and plans for Space Mountain were revived. From concept to creation Space Mountain took eleven years, but the attraction's popularity proves it was time well spent.

LOOK FOR

As you walk through the queue, look at the interplanetary route maps on your left-hand side. See if you can find Disney's Hyperion Resort and two Disney characters on the maps. *Hint:* The characters are Pluto and Ariel. It's a little bit of a cheat since Pluto actually was a planet, although it was downgraded to a dwarf planet, and Ariel is a moon hovering around Uranus. Still, it will give you something to talk about while you wait for your turn to ride.

Stitch's Great Escape!

Before Lilo met Stitch, he was a mischievous renegade terrorizing the universe. He has been caught and transported to the Galactic Federation to do time, and you're tasked with watching him. What could go wrong?

QUESTION I

Before you can work for the Galactic Federation, you need to know what your job entails. Luckily, a teleportation official is on hand to give you some instructions. Which California ZIP Code is the nickname of the Prisoner Teleportation Officer?

A 90013 (Los Angeles)

B 90210 (Beverly Hills)

C 95357 (Modesto)

D 92803 (Anaheim)

QUESTION 2

After Stitch is teleported into the containment tube, procedure dictates that he has to undergo a certain intake process. What process leads to the containment tube being opened and Stitch escaping?

_____

FASCINATING FACT

I'm not sure how fascinating this is, especially if you're sitting in one of the seats that end up being targets, but Stitch is in the exclusive club of Walt Disney World Audio-Animatronics characters that spit or otherwise shoot water. Others include the sneezing Brachiosaurus and spitting Ornithomimus at Epcot's Universe of Energy, the mayor in the well on Pirates of the Caribbean, and the elephants along Jungle Cruise. Stitch has the distinction of being able to speak as well.

LOOK FOR

During the short time the lights are on after Stitch escapes, you can track his movements on the overhead monitors.

Tomorrowland Speedway

On the farthest boundaries of Tomorrowland, you'll find old-fashioned racing. No hovercrafts here, just a chance for the kiddies to live out the dream of making rubber meet the road.

QUESTION I

Young guests can experience the thrill of racing, but first they have to pass a qualifying test. Drivers must be as tall as how many Astro Oil cans?

A Two

B Four

C Six

D Eight

QUESTION 2

Don't do it . . . DON'T DO IT . . . awww . . . you did it. At the end of your ride, you are asked to slow down and not do what?

FASCINATING FACT

What's a race track without its lap-counter tower? Tomorrowland Speedway hasn't forgotten this detail, and you'll be tempted to see if you beat everyone in your group as you zoomed (okay, puttered) around the track. But wait; look at the speeds posted. That can't be right! Now look at the laps. That can't be right either. It would be really cool if the placement indicators were correct, but sadly, the tower is just for show.

LOOK FOR

Car number 50 in Victory Circle sure does look familiar. With its two black headrests and its jaunty coat of red paint, it calls to mind a certain mouse when viewed from a distance, doesn't it? C'mon! You know it does!

Storybook Circus

This area re-decorates almost as often as the family in Carousel of Progress. It began as Mickey's Birthdayland, then became Mickey's Starland, and then it was Mickey's Toontown Fair, before opening as Storybook Circus in 2012, with settings based on the animated movie *Dumbo* and a few references to Disney animated short films.

QUESTION 1

The circus has come to town, and there are animals everywhere! Of course, with animals come animal tracks. Which animals did not leave their tracks in Storybook Circus?

A Giraffes

B Monkeys

C Camels

D Seals

QUESTION 2

Walt Disney's Carolwood Pacific Railroad is remembered in Storybook Circus on signs and on the clock outside the train station. What description of the area has been added to the clock?

FASCINATING FACT

The proximity of Storybook Circus and Fantasyland brings together the beloved classic cartoon characters with the high-tech Disney movie characters that today's children are enjoying.

Dumbo the Flying Elephant

Dumbo the Flying Elephant brings the gentle tale to life, wrapped up in a charming little elephant who reminds us to believe in ourselves. With the Disney touch, a simple fairground ride becomes a beloved childhood friend.

QUESTION I

Children love the thrill of flying with Dumbo, although they're more captivated by the sensation of flying than they are by the story being told on the ride's elaborate base. Which two characters from the movie feature prominently on the central tower?

A Timothy Q. Mouse and Mrs. Jumbo

B Mr. Stork and Mrs. Jumbo

C The Ringmaster and Timothy Q. Mouse

D The Ringmaster and Mrs. Jumbo

Dumbo achieves his dream of being accepted by the circus animals when he discovers and embraces his natural talent for flight. With that in mind, what is the inspirational advice given on the back of the sign as you exit the Dumbo area?

FASCINATING FACT

In the story, Dumbo finds his confidence when he believes a magic feather can make him fly. Magic feathers are a common thread in legends and folklore from around the world, symbolizing wisdom, change, and a connection to the divine.

LOOK FOR

As you fly with Dumbo, look at the paintings that tell his story. Notice one of the paintings references the pink elephant hallucinations Dumbo saw when he accidentally drank a bucket of water laced with Champagne. Is that another reason elephants can fly?

The Barnstormer

Barnstorming was once a popular feature of U.S. circuses, but Goofy may not be the best representative of the sport. He means well, but he spends less time focused on the fun and more time showing why stunt flying is so ridiculously dangerous.

QUESTION 1

Goofy is just . . . well . . . goofy! Never one to do things the ordinary way, Goofy used articles of clothing instead of a windsock. Which two items did he use?

A A shirt and boxer shorts

B A stocking cap and mittens

C Old boots and a parka

D A pair of pants and a pair of socks

QUESTION 2

Some of the items in the queue are nods to Disney animated short films. Each poster represents a Buena Vista Distribution Company film in which Goofy plays Mr. X. Which Disney short is referenced in the poster that shows Goofy waterskiing with an octopus on his head?

FASCINATING FACT

Inspiration for Goofy as a barnstormer at the former Wiseacre Farms came from a series of Disney short films in which Goofy plays different roles, from a fisherman to a baseball player to a dancer. It just seemed natural that he should expand his entrepreneurial tendencies to become the Great Goofini.

LOOK FOR

Goofy really puts himself into his work. Either that or he didn't really think things through when he peered down the neck of the cannon. Look at the target across the walkway. It seems Goofy's klutziness isn't a one-off; he's also flown through the red and white tower and the sign advertising his stupendous stunts.

Casey Jr. Splash 'N' Soak Station

In the animated movie *Dumbo*, Casey Jr. spends his time transporting circus animals from one location to the next. Here in Storybook Circus, he continues this noble work.

QUESTION 1

There's a whole lot of squirting going on, but unlike the camels, elephants, and giraffes, monkeys can't spit well enough to make it worthwhile. Instead, one clever monkey has resorted to a trick that gets the job done. What is it?

A He's wearing a squirting flower.

B He is shaking a big bottle of soda.

C He snorted snuff and is sneezing all over the place.

D He has a straw and a cup full of water.

QUESTION 2

They may have arrived in their own circus car, but that doesn't mean the monkeys are going to stay there! How did one clever monkey get from his car to the giraffes' car?

FASCINATING FACT

Casey Jr.'s day job is transporting circus animals, but at night he rubs elbows with the park's Big Cheese. As you're enjoying Main Street Electrical Parade, notice who is pulling the parade's sign, with Mickey and Minnie onboard, waving wildly to the crowd.

LOOK FOR

See those big bags of peanuts hanging from the elephants' circus car? Maybe it wasn't messy children who spilled peanuts all over the ground in Storybook Circus. The popcorn the birds are snapping up is real, of course; so we can't blame that on the elephants, now, can we?

MAGIC KINGDOM SCAVENGER HUNT

Magic Kingdom is full of fascinating gems, and this is your chance to uncover a few of them. Figure out the clues in each question, head to the area or attraction the clues suggest, and congratulate yourself for your super-sleuthing skills!

1. Baseball. Hot dogs. Apple pie. Quintessential American experiences, especially when the local team is playing. In which innings did Mudville score their two points?

2. Boys will be boys, and when Gaston invites friends to party with him, things get out of hand. How many arrows were shot during his last get-together, and how many hit the bull's-eye?

3. If you add up all the tusks, horns, and toenails along the avenue of gargoyles, what number do you get?

4. Columbia Harbour's residents and businesses honor their love of the ocean by decorating in all things nautical. Maps abound at Columbia Harbour House, as do remembrances of ships lost at sea. Go up a set of steps and there are several maps on the wall. One of the decorative items isn't a map. Which first-class clipper ship does this item mention?

5. Pecos Bill, a character from the 1948 Walt Disney classic *Melody Time*, has specific rules about how to act in front of women and children. Find the Code of the West posted on a wall. What is the third rule in the list?

6. Male deer are determined, and it appears they can climb buildings when it's time to shed their antlers. Or perhaps hunters from the shooting range had something to do with it, as decorating with antlers is quite

popular in the area. However, one location has more antlers than any other. If you add up the number of antlers that were shed, and assuming they are all from different bucks, how many deer were involved?

7. Franz Robinson has left a message about his family's misfortune, but he assures readers that things could be worse. They've salvaged what they could from the wreck and are making a good life on the island. When does Franz say they reached the site of their new home?

8. Pirates are tenacious, and this one hasn't given up his job as lookout, even though he has, apparently, been dead for years. Where is he and what is he looking at through his telescope?

9. In the future, even newspaper delivery is high-tech. Find the *Robo-News* and check out the headlines. There's trouble afoot, and it's all because of one pesky character. What is the caption under the headline feature's photo?

10. Aliens and humans live together harmoniously in the future; some might say they live in perfect harmony. With that in mind, where can you find "the biggest little star in the galaxy," and what color is his suit?

CHAPTER 2

Epcot

Explore the depths of the seas and the farthest reaches of space. Travel back in time and engineer the crops of the future. Feel the power of technology, the power of communication, and the power of the mind. Then, immerse yourself in the cultures of eleven different countries, all in the course of a day or two.

Think of Epcot not as the "educational" park, but as the park of discovery. Education is passive; discovery is where your own creativity and imagination come into play!

QUESTION 1

In some ways, Epcot started out as a true "city of the future" in that it couldn't stick to its budget. When the project began, estimates for a finished park were around $650 million. How much do some estimates indicate the final cost was?

A $800 million

B $900 million

C $950 million

D $1 billion

QUESTION 2

During the design stage, what issue prompted Imagineers to combine the models of Future World and World Showcase, which were originally intended to be two separate parks?

FASCINATING FACT

The monorail line running to Epcot was built at the same time the park was rising out of the ground, which also raised a dilemma: how to get the larger vehicles out of the park if they were too big to fit under the track. Solution? A section of the track near Spaceship Earth was left out, and it was only put into place once the last vehicle left the park.

LOOK FOR

Remember the **picture spots** you looked for at Magic Kingdom? All of the parks have them, so here's where to go at Epcot. You won't find photo spots at every pavilion, so at those pavilions that don't have designated spots, just line up your favorite view. Remember, the placement is described with you facing the camera.

- Stand directly in front of the landscaped central area when you first enter the park, with **Spaceship Earth** centered directly behind you.
- Sit directly under Dory in the character display to the left of the **Seas with Nemo & Friends** entry.
- At the **Imagination** pavilion, stand along the railing with the reverse waterfall behind you and the white pyramids over your left shoulder.
- In **China**, stand in front of the pond on the right side as you face the pavilion, then turn around so the Temple of Heaven is over your left shoulder and the contorted mulberry tree is to your right.
- **Germany's** best spot puts you on the patterned walkway at the pavilion's entrance, with the clock tower directly behind you.
- Cross the left-hand bridge leading to World Showcase lagoon, at the front of the **Italy** pavilion, and stand with the striped mooring poles behind you. Make sure the poles and gondolas are in your shot.
- Stand in front of the second chainlink fence to your right as you face World Showcase Lagoon, then turn around so that **Japan's** Torii Gate is behind and slightly off-center to the right of you.
- Stand just to the right of the first lamppost on the left side of the **Morocco** pavilion, with the main doorway to the Bab Boujeloud over your left shoulder.

- Stand in front of **France's** knot garden, on the right side as you face the pavilion, then turn around so that the Eiffel Tower and Palais du Cinema are just beyond your right shoulder.
- In the **United Kingdom**, stand on the sidewalk just in front of the curb with the right-hand corner of the thatch-roofed cottage behind you. The person holding the camera should be able to see the front of the cottage and the side of the cottage nearest the gardens.
- Stand halfway up the staircase leading into the **Canada** pavilion, with the dark brown totem pole just beyond your right shoulder.

Future World

If the back of the park is known as "a showcase of nations," the front of Epcot could rightly be called "a showcase of industry." Each pavilion explores modern-day challenges, offering solutions and prompting guests to ponder their own role in a better tomorrow. But, in best Disney style, very rarely do you realize there's a lesson in all the fun.

Spaceship Earth

Spaceship Earth was described as a journey of "civilization and communication from the Stone Age to the information age" by Bill Ellinghouse, president of AT&T, parent company of the attraction's opening-day sponsor, Bell Systems. To a degree, the pavilion still reflects this never-ending theme.

QUESTION I

During Spaceship Earth's last makeover, some scenes were improved by becoming animated rather than static. You'll notice this change right away when you reach the prehistoric scenes. According to Spaceship Earth's first scene, how many cavemen with big sticks does it take to slay a woolly mammoth?

A Three

B Four

C Five

D Twenty

Dame Judi Dench is the first woman ever to narrate the journey, and along the way she tells us we are poised to shape the future of . . . what?

FASCINATING FACT

In the post–Civil War scene, a man reads a newly printed newspaper whose headline shouts, "Civil War Over!" But what's wrong with this picture? Notice the newspaper is folded in half, and he's reading the bottom portion. If he really did that, and the paper's headline is upright as riders see it, the print he is viewing would be upside down.

LOOK FOR

A black handprint on the back wall in the Guttenberg printing press scene. It's obviously an Imagineer signature, since guests aren't allowed to slap their painted hands against attraction walls. Or is it the work of those prankster paleontology students over in Disney's Animal Kingdom's DinoLand U.S.A., who consider handprints a form of artistic expression?

The Seas with Nemo & Friends

Nemo is awfully hard to keep track of, in spite of the fact everyone is looking for him. Back when the pavilion was Sea Base Alpha, accessed by ingenious hydrolators and omnimover sea cabs, Epcot's educational focus on the ocean was obvious.

Now the little orange-and-white trickster puts the focus on fun, although it is possible you'll learn something in the process.

QUESTION I

The lifeguard manning tower 5A may not be in at the moment, but he's left an indication of today's sea conditions. What are they?

A Rockin' and Rollin'

B Just Swell

C Mercifully Mild

D Chompy!

QUESTION 2

By the time you leave the beach and head underwater for your clownfish search-and-rescue mission, that neglectful lifeguard still hasn't returned. How long does the sign on the back of his tower indicate he is supposed to be on duty?

FASCINATING FACT

Nemo and his friends can be found on signs, in animated form, and living among the pavilion's exhibits. But where in The Seas with Nemo & Friends can you find Nigel, the pelican hero in the movie *Finding Nemo*? Nowhere. He's the only main character not represented in the pavilion. However, he does make an appearance in the show, *Finding Nemo—The Musical*, over at Disney's Animal Kingdom.

LOOK FOR

When your ride vehicle reaches the first window into the aquarium, where Nemo, Marlin, and Dory are swimming, watch what happens when a live fish swims directly at them. Oh, the hazards of being animated!

The Land

Who knew agriculture was so interesting? From the ecological lessons of the Circle of Life to the hopeful advances toward a well-fed world promoted in Living with the Land, caring for the Earth is the main theme here. Then, you get a bird's-eye view of the beauty and diversity of this great nation (well, of California anyway), a reminder of what conservation efforts are all about.

QUESTION 1

A popular dining choice, the Garden Grill, a rotating restaurant, was formerly known as Land Grille Room. But that's not its original name. What was its name when the pavilion opened?

A Mickey's Marketplace

B Squat and Gobble

C Crop Circles

D Good Turn

QUESTION 2

Look up when you reach the atrium's balcony and you'll see a full year represented on four hot-air balloons. As seen from the balcony, between which two "seasons" balloons hanging from the atrium's ceiling does Florida (on the globe balloon) point?

FASCINATING FACT

Some of the produce used in both the Sunshine Seasons and Garden Grill restaurants was grown in the greenhouses you'll see during your Living with the Land journey. If you want to be sure you're eating something produced here, pick up a small container of coleslaw, tuna salad, pasta salad, or similar single-serving offering. While much of the produce used in both locations is sourced from vendors, the delicate lettuce leaves these items rest on began their lives in the attraction.

LOOK FOR

The landscaping on either side of the pavilion reflects the curving strata represented in the pavilion's outdoor mural and the undulating nature of lava flowing from its source. Notice the top portion of the pavilion is shaped to resemble a volcano? From this central point, the land is created, flowing out of the pavilion and coursing down either side. It is a pretty representation of one of the Earth's fundamental functions.

Living with the Land

This attraction garners some of the most interesting reactions, from "why doesn't everyone do this ride? It's brilliant!" to the guest who sailed through the greenhouses pointing out all of the plants that are used to create his favorite libations: "Look, honey, there's wheat and barley for beer, and over here you've got your agave and your lemon; just add tequila!"

QUESTION 1

No one can miss the rooster, who is crowing like there's no tomorrow. Other than that living wake-up call, which three common farm animals are featured in the farmhouse scene?

A Sheep, ducks, and a cow

B Chickens, goats, and a dog

C Chickens, goats, and piglets

D Goats, a cow, and a cat

QUESTION 2

If you add the number of buffalo, prairie dogs, and monkeys you see during your journey, what is the total?

FASCINATING FACT

During your tour of the greenhouse, you'll see banana plants. Did you ever wonder why they are curved? Look at the tip of the banana as you pass by. See that dried-up flower on the end? When the banana starts growing, the end with the flower is pointing down, but as the flower seeks more sunlight, it slowly pulls the banana into its curved shape. Neat, huh?

LOOK FOR

The automatic fish feeders in the aquaculture section. Although many innovations in food production displayed in Living with the Land have positive results, the automatic fish feeders are controversial when used at real-life open-water fish farms. Overfeeding increases fish-waste pollution and has a negative impact on native wildlife.

Soarin'

Soarin' over California debuted in Disney California Adventure Park in 2001, and then found its way to Walt Disney World as Soarin' in 2005. It has been Epcot's most popular attraction since the day the doors opened. Some of the highest praise I have heard came from an eighty-year-old man on his fifteenth ride. He had sent his family off to see the rest of Epcot while he spent his day happily hang-gliding over California.

QUESTION 1

Not only is your journey visually stunning, it smells good, too! Which scent is *not* "smellitzered" at you during your flight over California?

A Pine tree

B Dusty trail

C Sea spray

D Orange grove

QUESTION 2

You have plenty of company on your journey, from the fishermen in the streams below you to the skiers and mountain climbers on the hills you glide over to the horseback riders galloping through the canyons you're traversing. Which scene reveals you are not the lone hang glider?

FASCINATING FACT

You're winding your way through an airport. You pass by a version of security (if you're using FASTPASS, they even check your ticket). You stand in line waiting to board. You're instructed by a flight attendant to put your seat belt on and stow your belongings before your flight takes off. And then . . . you're hang-gliding! Wait, what? How did that happen!

The Circle of Life: An Environmental Fable

Timon and Pumbaa are about to learn a hard lesson, in spite of Mufasa's advice about respect for living things. Although environmental issues are much more graphic here than in the original *Lion King* movie, the message is the same: Nature exists in a delicate balance and the circle of life connects us all.

QUESTION I

Timon has always been a big fan of mottoes. What does he say the motto is for Hakuna Matata Lakeside Village?

A Vacation Where There Are No Worries

B The Savanna, but Better

C More! More! More!

D River Be Dammed

QUESTION 2

During the film, Timon uses three different names for Pumbaa and his grand resort, starting with Hakuna Matata Lakeside Village. What is the name Timon uses after he decides they have to think "way bigger" and before he finally settles on

Hakuna Matata All-Ecological Family Village Resort and Hog Wallow?

FASCINATING FACT
There is a pretty chant that is sung over and over in the "Circle of Life" song at the beginning of the show. What do those words mean? *Ingonyama nengw' enamabala* is Zulu and roughly translates to "a lion and a leopard (literally, 'a speckled one') come to this open place."

LOOK FOR
The stylized shafts of wheat represented on the carpeted walls as you wait for your show are mimicked in the mural at the loading area of Living with the Land, directly below you. A nice tie-up between two attractions with the same message, told in different ways.

Journey Into Imagination with Figment

Journey Into Imagination with Figment could be considered the ultimate Epcot pavilion, since the idea behind much of what the park represents is the power of human imagination. This pavilion has also been among the most controversial; it was imagined one way, then reimagined when guests felt it was a bit tired, then imagined all over again when guests cried out in agony over the loss of the characters Figment and Dreamfinder. Imagination is hard work!

QUESTION 1

Which two senses are not experienced during your tour of the Sensory Labs?

A Taste and touch

B Smell and taste

C Touch and smell

D Sight and sound

QUESTION 2

As you walk through the queue, several pages are broadcast over the lab's intercom system. At one point, all security personnel are being paged because something has been let loose and is running wild in Area 4. What is it?

FASCINATING FACT

Journey Into Imagination with Figment has gone by three different names, one of which reflects the somewhat disastrous removal of a beloved character. It began its life as Journey Into Imagination (1983), and then became Journey Into Your Imagination (1999) before making amends with guests by becoming Journey Into Imagination with Figment (2002).

Captain EO

Michael Jackson was here to change the world, or so his character, Captain EO, said. But they can't find the homing beacon, their map is gone, the crew is going to be turned into trash cans, and Captain EO is about to be punished with one hundred years of torture. How will he and his ragtag band of intergalactic innocents accomplish their mission? Through synchronized dance, of course!

QUESTION I

What is the name of Captain EO's boss?

A Supreme Commander

B Captain Crunch

C Admiral Anarchy

D Commander Bog

QUESTION 2

Captain EO has the key to unlocking the Supreme Leader's inner beauty. Not only will he let her see it, he'll let her hear it, too. But first he needs instruments. What is the second instrument he gets, and where does it come from?

FASCINATING FACT

Captain EO's ship has to crash-land on the Dark Planet. To achieve that effect, designers created a scaled-down landscape of industrial horror. The crew had to walk through this landscape as they filmed the scenes, so a trench was built into the set, giving the Dark Planet's major metropolis its name, Trench City. The landscape looks remarkably like the tunnel Luke Skywalker flew through just before blowing up the Death Star.

LOOK FOR

During the ship's crash landing, Captain EO is thrown to the floor. As he is lying there, he is pummeled by small bits of rubble and, inexplicably, ends up with a fried egg on his shoulder. The ship is absolutely trashed, but the fried egg remains perfectly intact.

Innoventions East and West

The original intent for Innoventions was to provide a place for guests to try out new and emerging technologies. Although an element of that idea remains, it could be argued the two pavilions now have a more sponsor-oriented theme.

QUESTION 1

Which savings strategy is not one of the Tips at the Great Piggy Bank Adventure?

A The whole family should be part of the plan.

B Understand the difference between "needs" and "wants."

C Save a little every month.

D Start saving early.

QUESTION 2

After a shaky start with an attraction that felt more insulting than inspiring, Disney switched gears, gave up the preachy spiel, and made healthy living fun. What better way for children to get behind a challenge than by turning them into superhero agents? Who are the Habitat Heroes that children are encouraged to emulate, and what do they battle against?

FASCINATING FACT

As you walk through the Innoventions buildings, look down at the floor. You're walking along the glittering Road to Tomorrow, which is paved with innovation and invention. Or, put simply, by innoventions. That's not the formal name of the road anymore; now it's a nameless road. But in 1999, when Sega Genesis 3 and Nintendo 64 were still making gamers swoon, the Road to Tomorrow was glitzy indeed.

Universe of Energy

Designed to "reflect" the energy of the universe, the mirrored walls at the front of the Universe of Energy often do just the opposite, especially in summertime when visitors use the hill on the opposite side of the walkway as a place to grab a quick nap. But the same cannot be said for the show inside. Ellen DeGeneres and Bill Nye brought liveliness to an attraction that was once a bit lethargic.

QUESTION 1

Today, the attraction in this pavilion is called Ellen's Energy Adventure. What was the short-lived title of the show that replaced the original Universe of Energy show?

A Ellen's Energy Crisis

B Energy, You Make the World Go 'Round

C The Universe: So Big It's Shocking!

D From Dino-juice to Natural Gas

QUESTION 2

Moving from fiery red to warm yellow, the colors on each side of the pavilion represent the intensity of energy, flowing from its center point at the front of the pavilion to its cooler form at the back of the pavilion. They also represent something else. It's an overriding theme throughout the dinosaur segment of the ride inside, but it's easy to miss as you're looking at the action around you. What is it?

FASCINATING FACT

That big structure outside the Universe of Energy is composed of the trylon (spire) and the perisphere (sphere). Although they have been placed together here and are holding the pavilion's sign, they were originally separate structures used as the icon for the 1939 World's Fair in New York.

LOOK FOR

See that textured bit of metal bolted to the right-hand corner of the reflection pool as you face the pavilion's sign? What earthly "energy" reason could it have for being there? None from the standpoint of the energy of the universe; you have to look at it from a duckling's point of view. This ramp is there to help ducklings get out of the water when they're too small to scramble out on their own. Most of the other ramps around the theme parks are temporary.

Ellen's Energy Adventure

Ellen's problem was the Universe of Energy's solution. Prior to the 1996 makeover, the world's energy issues were presented in a factual—and, let's face it, rather dry—way, prompting visitors to call it "the dinosaur ride" because the primeval forest segment was the only part they remembered. Today, a nice little nod to the former attraction's preshow song remains. Johnny Gilbert works its title into his commentary as Ellen writes out her *Final Jeopardy!* answer. He says, "Energy, you make the world go 'round."

QUESTION I

You have just survived the Big Bang and a crash landing on Earth. How far back in time does Bill Nye the Science Guy tell Ellen they have traveled?

A Back, back, back to the age of the dinosaurs.

B Billions of years, once the universe was born out of nothingness.

C Two hundred and twenty million years, give or take a day.

D To a time when Earth was the vast playground of the *Stegosaurus* and the *T. rex*.

QUESTION 2

What time period does Ellen want to visit to get out of having to deal with the dinosaurs Bill Nye thinks are so cool?

FASCINATING FACT

Although *Pteranodon* is a reptile not a dinosaur, it still makes an appearance in your dinosaur adventure. How do you know the genus here is a *Pteranodon* and not its cousin, the *Pterodactylus*, often wrongly called "pterodactyl"? The members of the *Pterodactylus* are smaller, they have teeth, and their skull is straight. The members of the *Pteranodon* are larger, have no teeth, and their skull curves dramatically upward.

LOOK FOR

Okay, so it's a movie and you're expected to cut it a little slack, but notice how Bill Nye the Science Guy runs off just before the Big Bang, virtually disappearing into the background. But when he rescues the hapless Ellen from being blown to smithereens, he pulls her through a doorway just steps away from where she was originally standing. Odd, isn't it?

Mission: SPACE

Whether you join in the astronaut-training program or not, it's hard to deny that this is one of Future World's most awe-inspiring pavilions, second only, perhaps, to Spaceship Earth. Most of the story is told in the courtyard's sculptures: You leave Earth (the blue planet), slingshot around the Moon (the gray body to the left), and rocket your way to Mars (the central dome). Why is Jupiter included? It's pretty big, it's Mars's nearest neighbor, and at one time, it helped guests avoid going up the FASTPASS ramp when they were really looking for the Standby entrance.

QUESTION 1

Who is quoted on a Mission: SPACE plaque as saying, "To confine our attention to terrestrial matters would be to limit the human spirit"?

A Albert Einstein

B Edwin Hubble

C Galileo

D Stephen Hawking

QUESTION 2

Inside the attraction, you'll find milestones in space history. Some of them are real, but some of them are there to support the idea that you're visiting in the year 2036. However, the milestones marked on the Moon to the left of the standby queue are all authentic. Which unmanned mission landed farthest from the first manned moon landing?

FASCINATING FACT

More than twenty years before the opening of Mission: SPACE, Disney was already imagining a space-themed pavilion centered around a mining company's base on an asteroid. As new recruits on a training mission, visitors would explore the space station, stroll around the asteroid, and plunge deep into its mines. The mining simulator would go from zero to sixty miles per hour in four and one-half seconds, exert three Gs of pressure, and slingshot around the asteroid three times. Sound familiar?

Mission: SPACE (the ride)

The dream of space flight becomes a reality—with all the attendant sensations zero gravity can produce, if you choose the intense version of the ride. The roles of Navigator, Pilot, Commander, and Engineer are played by guests, but (luckily) the real brains behind the mission comes from the onboard computer system, just in case you're so distracted by the experience that you forget to push the buttons and move the levers.

QUESTION 1
....

As you work your way through astronaut training in preparation for your mission, actor Gary Sinise introduces you to the spacecraft you will be manning. What is the name of this high-tech shuttle?

A X-2 Deep Space Shuttle

B REMO Deep Space Explorer

C Shuttle Nostromo

D Mars II Deep Space Explorer

QUESTION 2

Where have robotic teams at the International Space Training Center decided your landing site should be once you reach Mars?

FASCINATING FACT

You've been chosen to train for the first mission to Mars. Granted, your only real destination is inside a simulator, but isn't it interesting that when you arrive on the planet and escape a near-disastrous fate, you discover buildings, a convenient runway, and security barriers that have already been set up?

LOOK FOR

When you exit the attraction and enter the Advanced Training Lab, head to the Expedition Mars simulated game exhibit, directly across from Mission Space Race. Look in the first glass-fronted cabinet on the left-hand side of the gaming area. See that little yellow book tucked into the corner? Its title is *Expedition: Mars Noctis Labyrinthus*. We all know what Expedition Mars means, but *Noctis Labyrinthus* means "labyrinth of the night," the name given to a particularly maze-like series of valleys on the Red Planet.

Test Track Presented by Chevrolet

Formerly a high-energy spin around a General Motors proving ground as you tested the stamina of the latest in automotive technology, the ride was updated in 2012 to reflect its new sponsor, Chevrolet. There's an awful lot of blue in there now, and although the ride is loosely based on the original incarnation, each area you pass through is far less defined. Love the new version or not, popular consensus agrees: It has a certain *Tron*-like quality about it.

QUESTION 1

You will be speeding through some precarious places once your SIM Track testing begins, so you're going to need some high-tech help with navigation. Which system does your vehicle connect to when you reach the Capability Testing segment?

A Orbitron

B Garmin

C Magellan Roadmate

D OnStar

QUESTION 2

You know you've reached the Off-Road and Extreme Weather sequence when you see a flash of lightning, and you can't miss the twisting, turning curves of the Responsiveness Test. What special effect shows you're in the Aerodynamic Efficiency tunnel?

FASCINATING FACT

At Test Track 2.0, you're in the "digital realm" of design, rather than the real world. The original version of Test Track felt immediate, obvious, and interactive. Now, you're inside a computer looking at what works for your design and what doesn't. This is how modern engineers are able to test elements before the actual car is built. Sadly, this means no more heat lamps, freeze chambers, and barriers to crash into before you leave the computer world and hit the road for real.

LOOK FOR

As you're going through the Responsiveness Testing area, watch for some pretty wacky signs. See if you can spot the sign with two children crossing a road while holding an artist's palette, and the "squirrel crossing" sign that isn't really a squirrel. What is it? It's a beaver, in honor of Big Beaver Road (more commonly known as 16 Mile Road) in Michigan, where General Motors has their headquarters.

World Showcase

The World Showcase pavilions are a faithful, if incomplete, representation of eleven different countries that highlight their familiar personalities through well-known icons. They are a somewhat romanticized version of the truth, and therein lays their charm.

Mexico

Eat, drink, and be *muy alegre*; there's a festival in town! It's always dusk—the social hour—here in Mexico, and the vendors are out, the tequila is flowing, and if you head to the far left corner of the plaza, along the river winding past the ancient pyramid, you can attend the shortest concert in history.

QUESTION 1

What are the names of the three caballeros?

A Donald Duck, Speedy Gonzales, and José Feliciano

B Donald Duck, Slowpoke Rodriguez, and Baba Looey

C Donald Duck, José Carioca, and Panchito

D Donald Duck, Toodles Galore, and Ciro Peraloca

QUESTION 2

Banners adorn the plaza in celebration of the upcoming concert given by the Three Caballeros. What is the Spanish word for these festive little papers?

Gran Fiesta Tour Starring the Three Caballeros

Donald, Donald, Donald. He's a troublemaker, but a loveable troublemaker. With a little help from his friends—and you!— he might just make it to tonight's concert. But first, you have to chase him all over Mexico.

QUESTION I

What grows along the shoreline as you pass the Mayan temple during your river journey?

A Cattails and water lilies

B Palm trees and Spanish moss

C Bamboo and bougainvillea

D Bougainvillea and cattails

Which three items are on the beach towel in Donald's Cancún scuba-diving scene?

FASCINATING FACT

The Three Caballeros are performing in concert as part of a big Fiesta Hoy ("party today") for the Day of the Dead, which remembers deceased loved ones. The festival has its origins in Aztec ritual, celebrating the transition from the "dream state" of living to the "awake state" of the afterlife. While visiting the graves of their dearly departed, relatives leave useful items for the souls to enjoy in the great beyond. Toys are left for departed children and a bottle of tequila is considered an appropriate gift for adults.

LOOK FOR

When you enter the first tunnel, look at the painting on the right. There's a Mayan who looks as if he's trying to pick a fight with the guy in front of him. You might want to snap a quick picture so you can enjoy the full outrage when you get home.

Norway

Norway is the "new kid on the block," arriving eight years after Epcot opened, but it's a fan favorite, in part because there's a ride and in part because there are princesses, but mostly because Vikings and trolls are just cool.

QUESTION 1

Disney's creative touch is evident not only in the attractions, but also in the signage around the parks. Which two elements make up the sign for Kringla Bakeri Og Kafe?

A A puffin and a salmon

B A polar bear and an iceberg

C A Viking ship and a sword

D A crown and a pretzel

QUESTION 2

Two mythical beasts can be seen on the large wooden panels at the back of the pavilion near the restrooms. Which two animals are melded to form the beast on the left panel?

FASCINATING FACT

Mmmmm . . . the Norway smell! If you've been to World Showcase before, you know what I mean. If you haven't, you'll never forget it once you smell it. The Polynesian resort has a unique smell (wet soil); and Splash Mountain in Magic Kingdom has its own smell (musty). In Norway it's due to excessive spraying of the pavilion's featured perfume line, Laila. As you walk around the park, you'll catch a whiff of it on a passing tourist and say, "Mmmmm . . . Norway!" Trust me on this one.

Maelstrom

This ride is named for the massive whirlpools that form after a tsunami or when opposing currents collide. Maelstrom is also synonymous with "chaos." In popular literature, maelstroms tend to occur when a situation has turned to bedlam. Still want to take the ride? Go on then! Be sure to give six minutes of your time to the short travelogue at the end. It's really quite interesting.

QUESTION I

How many polar bears can be seen from the time you enter your Viking longship to the time you exit it?

A Two

B Five

C Six

D Eight

QUESTION 2

Maelstrom's queue may not be as interactive and exciting as some, but it does include an interesting historical element. What is the title of the giant map on the right-hand wall as you walk through the queue?

FASCINATING FACT

The mural in the boarding area is a sneak peek at what you're about to see as you journey through Norwegian fact and fantasy. In particular, note the people tending a campfire, the polar bears, oil rigs, lightning, and the pine tree—covered troll. You'll even see sailboats and a quaint village with a lighthouse at the end of your boat journey.

LOOK FOR

As soon as you enter the first lift hill area, look to your left. There are animal figures carved into the rockwork, just about at eye level. See if you can identify a fish, a reindeer, a Viking ship, and some hunters. You'll have to look quickly!

China

Among the oldest civilizations in the world, and with a population exceeding 1 billion, China places great value on inward pursuits and the beauty of serenity. Those ideals can be seen in abundance in the China pavilion. From the tranquil ponds to the tight, bustling Xing Fu Jie (literally, Fortune Street), symbolism is everywhere.

QUESTION 1

Foo Dogs—or, more accurately, Shishi, meaning "stone lion"—are a common decorative element in China, often appearing outside shops and restaurants. The female Foo rests her paw on a cub; the male Foo holds down a ball. Nearly always seen together, what concept do they represent?

A Passiveness and Power

B Tolerance and Conviction

C Yin and Yang

D Life and Death

QUESTION 2

In China, a five-clawed dragon signifies the emperor's property, the empress uses a phoenix, but the common people tend to use their own names on their buildings. What is the name of the proprietor of Lotus Blossom Cafe and Nine Dragons restaurants?

FASCINATING FACT

The tiles on the Temple of Heaven in Epcot are not painted, glazed, and kiln-fired, as would be traditional; instead, they are screen-printed. What's screen-printing? It's a process similar to silk-screening, using mesh, a stencil, and a squeegee. In this way, many tiles can be produced quickly.

Reflections of China

Wonders of China, the original show found in China, focused on the history of this country and its natural wonders. Many of the same elements were used in *Reflections of China*, in a different order, and new scenes were added to reflect the modern face of this vast country.

QUESTION 1

Modern China is busy and bustling, filled with big-city drive and determination. Amid all that chaos, what does your host, Li Bai, indicate there is always time for in China?

A Tai chi

B Hot tea

C Poetry

D Kimchee

QUESTION 2

Li Bai also says China's history is not written in ink, but with . . . what?

___

FASCINATING FACT

Some of the scenes shot for the *Wonders of China*, and also used in *Reflections of China*, were the first glimpses the Western world had of these hidden, if well-known, locations.

LOOK FOR

Precision and beauty are important aspects of Chinese life. As you are facing forward during the movie, look over your right shoulder and watch for the man scraping noodles from a block of dough into a pot of boiling water. These are *dao xiao mian* (knife-shaved noodles), and while he makes it looks easy, give it a try at home some time. Once you have the technique mastered, it's fun to watch the noodles fly!

Germany

Get your oom-pah-pah on, we're going to Germany! It could be argued this is the most romanticized pavilion in World Showcase, a charming representation of the gingerbread style of Bavaria, grounded by the strength of a solid German castle.

QUESTION 1

The wall across from the Sommerfest quick-service counter is painted to look like a tapestry featuring an idyllic compilation of the Rothenberg Road, which goes by another, more popular name. What is its alternate name?

A Romantic Road

B Wine Way

C Magical Miles

D Riverview Road

QUESTION 2

Freiburg, Germany's merchant house displays the figures of Maximilian I, his son, Philip, and Philip's sons, Charles V and Ferdinand I. Maximilian didn't make the cut at Epcot's Germany due to space restrictions, but Philip, Charles, and Ferdinand are here. What do these three Hapsburg princes have directly above their heads?

FASCINATING FACT

The architectural style of Das Kaufhaus is mimicked in the pretty train display to the right of the Germany pavilion. Look at the center set of houses on the lower level, and you'll see a tan building resembling the side façade of Kaufhaus, a sixteenth-century merchant hall in Freiburg, the building Epcot's Das Kaufhaus is based on.

Italy

You have to love a country that comes up with proverbs like *L'acqua ti fa sentire male e il vino fa cantare* ("Water makes you feel bad and wine makes you sing"). If you don't have time to sample some of Italy's famous wines, take a sip from the water fountain as you make your way toward American Adventure and say, *"Alla Salute"* ("to your health"). Don't worry if you can't remember it. It's written in the fountain's tile work.

QUESTION I

· ·

All of the World Showcase pavilions are an amalgam of the countries they represent rather than being one specific region. Which geographical region in Italy does the Enoteca Castello wine shop represent?

A Sicily

B Calabria

C Tuscany

D Lazio

QUESTION 2

Italy is famous, in part, for its beautiful Murano glass. Which four fruits are found in glass form, hanging from the chandelier in the lobby of Via Napoli?

FASCINATING FACT

The central plaza is reminiscent of the plazas that define neighborhoods in Italian urban centers. Here it is appropriately called Plaza del Teatro, meaning "theater plaza." From the time the pavilion opened, it has hosted live street entertainment, including mimes, strolling musicians, and the long-gone but wildly popular Living Statues.

LOOK FOR

On the right-hand side of the pavilion, after the wine shop but before the fountain of Neptune, you'll see a door with columns on either side. The columns are a timeline of sorts, representing the Classical Orders of column architecture. On the bottom are Doric columns, the earliest style created by the Greeks and adopted by the Romans, associated with strength and masculinity for their bulky, weight-bearing attributes. Next are Ionic columns, a more feminine style added between 570 and 560 B.C.E., and finally, Corinthian columns with their elaborately carved capitals (tops). Corinthian columns became popular in 450–420 B.C.E. and remain a favored style in modern design.

The American Adventure

The American Adventure does not tell the history of the United States, rather it focuses on pivotal issues as the country developed, beginning with the founding of the first settlement. Why were Benjamin Franklin and Mark Twain chosen as the hosts for this attraction? They were "the voices of their times" and both were well known for their sense of humor.

QUESTION 1

When Epcot was built, pavilions had sponsors that usually had something to do with the pavilion's theme. Which former sponsor of The American Adventure still has an advertisement in the Great Depression segment of the show?

A Ford Motor Company

B Coca-Cola

C Exxon Mobil

D Kodak

QUESTION 2

Which main character in The American Adventure show is not based on a real historical figure?

FASCINATING FACT

Although Imagineers were painstakingly dedicated to authenticity in creating The American Adventure, the phosphorous flash of the camera during the Americans Divided scene is not accurate to the times. It was used as a visual device to transition into the "Two Brothers" song.

LOOK FOR

See that old ship docked behind the American Gardens Theatre? It's not the *Mayflower*; it's the *Golden Dream*, a replica of the Virginia sloops used during the Revolutionary War for trading with islands off the U.S. coastline. The name, seen on the back of the ship, is derived from the theme song for The American Adventure.

Japan

Epcot's Torii Gate is modeled after the gate found in Hiroshima Bay outside the Itsukushima Shrine, a UNESCO World Heritage site; its pagoda is based on Horyuji Shrine at Nara; and its main shop is based on Mitsukoshi, Japan's oldest department store. The pavilion is best enjoyed at a slow, contemplative pace, ideally with a Kakigōri shaved ice treat in hand.

QUESTION I

There is something funky about those fish on the rooftops. Which two animals make up the head and the tail?

A The head is a dragon; the tail is a peacock.

B The head is a sea serpent; the tail is a dolphin.

C The head is a dragon; the tail is a fish.

D The head is a barracuda; the tail is a carp.

QUESTION 2

Design elements have great symbolism in Japan, and they are used throughout the pavilion. What well-known symbol is used as a decorative element on the ends of the fortress's blue roof tiles?

_____

FASCINATING FACT

Japanese gardens were originally utilized only by the ruling class to gain clarity and peace of mind during times of conflict. Then the military elite began adding gardens to the land they were granted as a reward for a job well done, and finally, business-people planted these gardens as a symbol of wealth and status. Not until the twentieth century were traditional gardens open to the public. Here in Epcot's Japan, two types of gardens are represented: the dry garden in front of Mitsukoshi and the tea garden surrounding the Katsura Grill. The dry garden is intended for reflective contemplation, while a stroll through the tea garden provides tranquility before a tea ceremony.

LOOK FOR

See those Japanese letters above the fortress's entry that leads to the Kidcot station and the Bijutsu-kan Gallery? They are written using the Hiragana alphabet and they spell out *ko n ni chi ha*. What does *konnichiha* mean? It means, "Hello," and it's okay to pronounce it *Ko-nee-chee-wah* when you greet a Japanese Cast Member.

Morocco

Think of the Moroccan pavilion, and its elaborate tile work is probably among the first images that come to mind. Nineteen *maalems* (artists) were brought to Epcot to ensure authenticity in the pavilion, with each tile placed just so in their re-creation of Morocco's famous icons.

QUESTION 1

You'll find Arabic words all around the Morocco pavilion, most of their meanings may not be obvious in relation to their locations. The Arabic sign above the door leading to the character meet and greet, just across from Restaurant Marrakesh, is roughly translated as

A "Place of worship."

B "The house of the poet."

C "Have your autograph book ready."

D "Welcome to the marketplace."

QUESTION 2

Morocco's marketplaces are fairly authentic, but with an addition that makes them more comfortable when Florida's weather turns wild. Why don't you get wet while strolling the market stalls of the outdoor bazaar?

France

Although World Showcase pavilions are a combination of several areas within the individual countries, France's pavilion is profoundly Parisian. With the benefit of a movie that takes you all around this beautiful country, the pavilion could afford to concentrate primarily on its most popular city.

QUESTION 1

La Petit Rue may be a small street, but it's big enough to support several businesses. Which one is not represented along this little avenue?

A La Casserole

B L'Esprit de la Provence

C Soleil et Lavande

D Boulangerie Hachoir á Viande

QUESTION 2

An art nouveau archway leading to the Métro station at Porte Dauphine in Paris has been recreated in Epcot's France, modeled on the elegant work of Hector Guimard. Where can you find the distinctive glasslike petals on a green metal arch?

FASCINATING FACT

What's with the green boxes on the wall at the extreme front of the pavilion? They represent Les Bouquinistes; riverside vendors who set up shop along the Seine in heavily trafficked tourist areas, selling the used books that gave them their name (*bouquiniste* means "bookseller"). Their noble trade dates back to the 1500s; it is such a popular career choice that the wait times to own the iconic green boxes can be nearly a decade.

LOOK FOR

See that beautiful clock in the knot garden that's all lovely and French-like? Look at the name of the company that created it, just above where the clock's hands are attached. It was made by the Verdin Company of Cincinnati, Ohio. Not very *belle époque*, is it? But wait . . . if you work hard for it, there is a tenuous tie to France. Verdin and a French company called Paccard Fonderie in Annecy-le-Vieux both create castings of bells. Paccard was the company that cast the Liberty Bell in Magic Kingdom's Liberty Square. Neat little tie-up, isn't it?

Impressions de France

China has gone from wondering to reflecting and Mexico gave the boot to its 1980s-style "visit Cancún" travelogue in favor of cartoon characters. But France . . . France's impressions are as timeless as the music that defines her countryside and cityscapes, as breathtaking today as they were when the show opened in 1982.

QUESTION 1

The peppy music of Offenbach's *Gaîté Parisienne* in the La Roque-Gageac bicycling scene probably doesn't help the situation, but which animal has an almighty freak-out when a group of cyclists go whizzing by?

A A sheep

B A goat

C A dog

D A squirrel

QUESTION 2

If you've ever had a glass of fine French wine, you won't forget the end result of the grape harvest, here depicted at Monbazillac Vineyard. What has the tractor driver done that shows he's already in a celebratory mood?

_____

FASCINATING FACT

The grand symphonic strains played during the final Eiffel Tower scene at the end of the *Impressions de France* film comes from Camille Saint-Saëens' Symphony Number 3 in C Minor, or the Organ Symphony. It's also the music used in adapted form in the 1995 hit movie *Babe*, sung by the mice while Farmer Hogget dances for the unhappy piglet. You'll never hear it the same way again, will you?

LOOK FOR

In scene six, as the church bells in Vézelay Abbey cease chiming, you are riding in a hay cart; look to the far-left screen. You can see the reflection of the trolley and the cameraman passing by the window as they film the hay cart moving along the street.

United Kingdom

France relies heavily on Paris for its settings, but the United Kingdom is all over the place—and all across time. High Street is a mixture of Elizabethan, Tudor, and Victorian buildings; Belgrave Square represents Hyde Park, Yorkshire, and Regency; and, of course, that castle at the front belongs to none other than King Henry VIII. It's his palace of Hampton Court.

QUESTION 1

Who is holding the medieval coats of arms on the upper balcony in the Historical Research Center next to the Crown & Crest?

A Two knights in suits of armor

B Queen Victoria and Prince Albert

C Winnie-the-Pooh and Tigger

D A medieval knight and his lady fair

QUESTION 2

Red phone booths are iconic of England . . . postboxes, not so much. Even so, you'll find one mailbox next to the phone booths at the front of the pavilion and one tucked away at the back of the pavilion. On which two days is the mail not collected from these postboxes?

FASCINATING FACT

The postbox near the Toy Soldier comes from a somewhat historical area of Yorkshire. Charlotte Brontë, author of *Jane Eyre*, was born in Thornton.

LOOK FOR

Check out house number 3 on Upper Regency Street. Then turn the corner to see what should be the left side of the house. Instead, it's house number 33. If it were real, the doorway would lead straight into the landing of house number 3. Most of these dual-use buildings work well, as evidenced by the Edwardian style of the columned white building to the left of the gazebo, and its postwar London counterpoint on the opposite side, facing the gardens. Here at house number 3, however, the transition is somewhat startling.

Canada

From the fables told by the First Nation people to the majestic Canadian Rockies, this pavilion tells a rugged tale of loggers, trappers, miners, and that burliest of professions, hoteliers.

QUESTION 1

Fences around World Showcase Lagoon aren't all that fancy, but there is an exception. Which icon has been carved into the fence posts along the waterside at the Canada pavilion?

A A moose head

B A hockey stick

C A maple leaf

D A loon

QUESTION 2

There are three enormous totem poles outside Northwest Mercantile, but they're not the only ones in Canada. How many totem-style poles does the pavilion have, including the three giant ones?

FASCINATING FACT

How many brawny lumberjacks did it take to hoist the big, dark brown totem pole into place? Fewer than you might think. Walk around the back of the pole and look up. It's actually only half a totem pole.

O Canada!

Enter through the Maple Leaf Mine, where picks, shovels, and oil lanterns adorn the walls. Although mineral prospecting is never mentioned in the movie, it's a clever setting honoring Canada's 350 years of mining history.

QUESTION 1

What misconception about Canada is Martin Short trying to dispel during the show?

A Everyone in Canada says "eh" at the end of every sentence.

B Joining a hockey team or the Mounties is compulsory.

C It snows for twelve months, and the country is filled with eagles and polar bears.

D Canadians drink maple syrup by the glass-full.

QUESTION 2

It's so popular it's included on their money! Which famous boat is featured in O Canada! and on the Canadian dime?

FASCINATING FACT

The first three notes of the Canadian National Anthem have been woven into the song "Canada, My Canada." Listen for the trumpet at the very end, honoring the attraction's namesake song.

LOOK FOR

As you make your way toward the entry to *O Canada!* look for a rock on your left that seems out of place. It's more like a fat, squashed mud pie than a rock. If you look closely, you'll notice the word *Water* is carved into it. It's actually the cover for the emergency shutoff valves for the waterfalls you see to your right.

IllumiNations: Reflections of Earth

A magnificent piece of engineering, Earth Globe displays a succession of images from prehistoric forests and seas, to cultural landmarks, to ordinary people, to famous artists, writers, and musicians, to political and industrial figures. Its musical score blends the rhythms of world cultures, culminating in an inspiring finale that almost takes your breath away.

QUESTION 1

How many technicians does it take to run the nightly *IllumiNations* show?

A 3   **B** 5   **C** 7   **D** 10

QUESTION 2

From how many locations are the 2,800 shells used in each show launched?

FASCINATING FACT

Audio specialist Don Dorsey directed *IllumiNations*, and also helped develop Main Street Electrical Parade.

LOOK FOR

Walt Disney. Of all the dreamers and doers honored on the IllumiNations globe, you can probably agree that Walt holds a well-deserved place among the honorees and a special place in our hearts.

EPCOT SCAVENGER HUNT

Epcot is known as the "innovations park," so tap into your spirit of adventure and see how many clues you can turn into discoveries!

1. Dr. Nigel Channing has a lot of responsibility at the Institute. What is his fourth job title and where is it found?

2. If the average Italian drinks ten bottles of wine per month, how many months would it take for them to make one overhead light fixture in Tutto Gusto?

3. During the Tang Dynasty, double-humped camels were believed to be used by the deceased to transport their goods in the afterlife. Where can you find a small representation of this noble animal?

4. A very special plaque traveled into space with Space Shuttle *Atlantis* on April 24, 2000. Where can you find it and to whom is it dedicated?

5. Where can you find an intricate carving that weaves a ship, a sword in its sheath, the face of a bearded king, and a bird into its pretty knotted design?

6. You expect to find moose in Canada, but which other World Showcase pavilion also displays a moose skull and antlers, and where are they located?

7. The four-clawed dragon is a symbol of power deemed acceptable for display by commoners, while the five-clawed dragon is reserved for the use of the emperor. But there is another dragon the average person is allowed to display. Where at the Lotus Blossom Cafe have the owners decided to use the three-clawed dragon?

8. Why settle for a tiny Eiffel Tower when you could own a map of Paris from the year 1575? Interested? You'll have to find it first.

9. Where can you find the proverb "The first thing one should own is a home; and it is the last thing one should sell, for a home is one's castle this side of heaven."

10. It's just too wacky to be true, and yet . . . if you search for them, you'll find a trophy cup for the Grand Champion Milking Cow and the Highest Scoring Chicken in Show. Who were the winners of these trophies, respectively?

CHAPTER 3

Disney's Hollywood Studios

The heavens opened up for two and a half hours during the 1989 opening-day events at Disney-MGM Studios, causing generators powering the lights set up for the evening events to shut down. But Disney remained undaunted. Out came the hair dryers, and an hour later it was Lights, Camera, Action! Inspired by a desire to showcase real moviemaking, the park, which changed its name to Disney's Hollywood Studios in 2008, has evolved to officially include film, animation, television, music, and theater, creating an all-around entertainment experience. And now, on with the show!

QUESTION 1

Magic Kingdom, Epcot, and Disney's Animal Kingdom rely heavily on popular animated-movie characters to flesh out the in-park experience. But Disney's Hollywood Studios is different. Although you'll meet your Disney movie friends too, which characters are the real stars (or, at least, star-wanabees) of the park?

A The Citizens of Hollywood

B The Hollywood Hucksters

C The Starlet Cavalcade

D Mr. DeMille's Dollies

QUESTION 2

Most of the buildings in Disney's Hollywood Studios are based on real locations in California. Two of them are based on a style that became popular as travel by car increased and business owners wanted a quick way to catch the attention of the traveling public. Dinosaur Gertie is one example of "California crazy" architecture. Which building as you enter Disney's Hollywood Studios is a second example?

FASCINATING FACT

Mann's Chinese Theater is the stand-out icon in Hollywood Studios, Sorcerer's Hat notwithstanding, but there is something unique about it as it relates to the other architecture in the park. The façade was based on Grauman's Chinese Theatre's actual blueprints and is the only building in the park that was built to full scale.

LOOK FOR

By now you know what to look for, right? Surprisingly, considering it's a park that's all about moving pictures, there aren't many established still-picture spots. But you won't have any trouble finding photogenic places worth adding to the list. Here are the "official" Hollywood Studios picture spots:

- Stand in the middle of **Hollywood Boulevard** at the point where you see the first planter (located behind the building with the wait-times list, to the right of the Hollywood Brown Derby). Stand with the restaurant to your left and Mickey's *Fantasia* hat centered behind you.
- Stand outside **Animation Courtyard** with the Hollywood Studios arch directly behind you and the lamppost at the end of the walkway in front of the Hollywood Brown Derby to your left.
- Stand with the body of the giant guitar outside **Rock 'n' Roller Coaster Starring Aerosmith** directly behind you. Do your best rock star pose!
- Stand to the left side of **Star Tours—The Adventures Continue** with the AT-AT walker directly behind you.

Hollywood Boulevard

Hollywood's up-and-coming actors and producers hang out here, amid architecture that would be familiar to real-life stars of the 1930s and 1940s. While the real buildings are not all grouped together like this, Disney's Hollywood Boulevard is still a pretty convincing start to the show.

QUESTION 1

Art deco buildings, movie-actor wannabes, and the grand old songs of Hollywood's heyday surround you. Wonderful details, large and small, abound, some of them quite whimsical. What is the shape of the sign attached to Disney & Co.?

A A Mickey Mouse wristwatch

B A playbook from the movie *Snow White*

C A musical note

D An open locket with pictures of Cinderella and Prince Charming

QUESTION 2

One of moviemaking's cuddliest stars made his start as an actor in the 1930 Disney short, *The Chain Gang*, assisting prison guards when Mickey Mouse escaped during a riot. Which beloved Disney character now has his own shop on Hollywood Boulevard, and what is it called?

The Great Movie Ride

When Disney-MGM Studios opened, The Great Movie Ride was the feature attraction, encompassing the overall concept the park wanted to convey: that this wasn't just a theme park, it was a dynamic moviemaking mecca. Not only could you "ride the movies," you were also placed right in the middle of the action.

QUESTION 1

In the Indiana Jones scene, your tram driver is intent on stealing the priceless jewel imbedded in the "great stone god." As your guide reaches for it, the guardian of the jewel warns against disturbing the treasure of the gods. What are you told will happen if the guide's greed wins out?

A The wrath of Osiris shall rain down upon you!

B It will all get ugly from here!

C You shall all pay with your lives!

D You shall be entombed forever!

QUESTION 2

In the first gangster scene, featuring James Cagney as Tom Powers in the movie *The Public Enemy*, Powers is looking for his former-mentor-turned-coward. What is the name of the person Powers says he is looking for?

FASCINATING FACT

Contrary to the incorrect date on the plaque outside the Great Movie Ride, Grauman's Chinese Theatre in Hollywood celebrated its grand opening on May 18, 1927, and its official opening to the public on May 19, 1927. Perhaps the signmaker confused Mann's debut with Mickey's debut as Steamboat Willy, which *did* occur in 1928.

LOOK FOR

When Sid Grauman's Chinese Theatre opened, a happy accident in which a star stepped in a bit of the courtyard's wet cement led to the famous handprints and footprints that adorn the Los Angeles version. As you wander the courtyard in Disney's Hollywood Studios, look for a set of prints made posthumously. Besides those prints "made" by fictional movie characters such as R2-D2 or Goofy, rather than the person who plays the character, Judy Garland's ruby slippers from the movie *The Wizard of Oz* are the only prints that weren't made by the person they honor.

Sunset Boulevard

When the park opened, Sunset Boulevard ended at . . . well . . . Hollywood Boulevard. Hard as it is to imagine now, the street did not exist until 1994. But when it opened, what a dramatic difference it made to a relatively tame theme park!

QUESTION I

As you round the corner of Hollywood Boulevard and Sunset Boulevard, you'll see the Pacific Electric building on your right, home to the iconic Red Car Trolley. What is Pacific Electric's motto?

A A ride so smooth it's shocking!

B Comfort, Speed, Safety.

C Friendliest conductors in Hollywood.

D With Pacific Electric, your ride is in the red.

QUESTION 2

At one time, Sunset Boulevard was going to have a trolley ride based on the movie *Who Framed Roger Rabbit*. Now they just have a red car trolley gift kiosk. What areas does Trolley 694, near the Hollywood Tower Hotel, serve?

FASCINATING FACT

Before the arrival of Sunset Boulevard, a giant "hidden Mickey" was clearly visible on the park map. Imagine Mickey's full, smiling face, with his mouth where the Chinese Theater is, his left ear made from Echo Lake lagoon, and his right ear partially created from the pavement on what is now Sunset Boulevard and partially painted on the roof of what is now the soundstage for Disney Junior—Live on Stage! Even though Mickey's face is no longer there, you can still follow part of the "hidden Mickey" by walking the circle of pavement around Echo Lake lagoon, or walking along the gray pavement in front of the Great Movie Ride, which is the remaining, but slightly modified, outline of Mickey's smile.

LOOK FOR

You're in 1940s Hollywood, and naturally the locals are eager to support the troops overseas. Look for evidence of their patriotism, such as the recruitment posters on the right side of the Villains in Vogue shop, and the mailbox that urges citizens to buy war bonds and stamps.

Beauty and the Beast—Live on Stage

Beauty and the Beast—Live on Stage is the now-familiar story told in magnificent style, worthy of a Broadway production. Unlike the other attractions along Sunset Boulevard, *Beauty and the Beast—Live on Stage* is all about the fairy-tale element of moviemaking.

QUESTION I
....

The Prince—who goes only by the name Prince or Beast in the original story and in the Disney movie—has eyes only for Belle.

However, there is one slight exception. What does the Beast do at the end of the show?

A He comes into the audience and waltzes with a female volunteer.

B He blows kisses to all of the ladies at court.

C He gives a rose to a young audience member.

D He winks knowingly at the witch.

QUESTION 2

A talented cast performs most of the musical numbers throughout the show, with a few exceptions. Who sings as Belle sees her prince in human form for the first time?

FASCINATING FACT

In the 362-page original story, *La Belle et la Bête*, written by Gabrielle-Suzanne Barbot de Villeneuve, Belle's father is a wealthy merchant with six sons and six daughters, who loses his fortune through a series of mishaps. While her vain sisters cry for jewels and pretty dresses, Beauty asks only for a single rose. When her father picks a rose at an enchanted castle, Beast forgives the transgression with the merchant's promise that one of his daughters will surrender her freedom willingly. Only Beauty is willing to do so. While she is Beast's captive, she dreams of a prince, never realizing he is the Beast. Beast lies dying when he fears Beauty has abandoned him, but she returns from visiting her father using a magical ring and agrees to marry Beast. Through Beauty's selflessness, Beast is restored to his true form as a handsome prince. Quite a different story, isn't it?

The *Twilight Zone* Tower of Terror

1939 is the year. The Golden Age of Hollywood is the setting. Halloween night is the date and 8:05 P.M. is the time. The thirteenth floor of a twelve-floor hotel is your destination. Or is it? No, my friend, your destination is (say it with me . . .) the Twilight Zone.

QUESTION 1

Which slogan was never used for the Tower of Terror?

A Never the Same Fear Twice.

B It's a Snap!

C The Tower Is in Control.

D Fear Every Drop!

QUESTION 2

The Hollywood Tower Hotel is one of the most detailed, immersive settings of any Disney attraction. You'll probably wish you could skip the ride—just once—and wander through the lobby for a good look at the individual settings. Until then, what popular game were four of the hotel's guests playing in the lobby at the time the hotel was struck by lightning?

FASCINATING FACT

Don't annoy the bellhops or they might retaliate by giving you more of a ride than you bargained for. Or will they? What criteria do Cast Members use to decide how many drops each elevator will make? They don't. Computers control the random drop sequences, meaning, the tower is in control!

LOOK FOR

When you exit the gift shop at the end of your journey into the unknown, catch your breath and turn around. The courtyard you're standing in gives you a fantastic view of the incredible architectural details the Imagineers put into this attraction. You can also get a vague idea of the ride track from here. Your elevator car starts at the back of the building, ascends, and then moves forward into the drop shaft. After a few harrowing drops, guests unload at the front of the building. The ride vehicle (elevator car) then returns, empty, to the back of the building, where it picks up a new batch of unsuspecting visitors.

Rock 'n' Roller Coaster Starring Aerosmith

Everyone knows Aerosmith will do anything for their fans, because that's the kind of guys they are. Today, they've ordered a superstretch limo for a rockin' trip across town, where your backstage passes are waiting.

QUESTION I

It's big, it's red, and it would take a huge, huge star to play it if it were real. What brand is the giant guitar outside the ride?

A Les Paul
B Gibson
C Ibanez
D Fender

QUESTION 2

Your trip from the recording studio to the Los Angeles Civic Center is unlike any you've ever taken. Predictably, there's a problem. What's wrong with the highway, and what are you instructed to do to solve the problem?

FASCINATING FACT

This attraction opened in time for Disney's Millennium Celebration and has been blasting Aerosmith music into riders' ears ever since. But Aerosmith wasn't the first band Disney approached. Their first choice was the Rolling Stones. The Stones heard a loud "cha-ching!" and said yes. When Disney heard their asking price, the Stones heard a loud no. Aerosmith, obviously, was far more reasonable.

LOOK FOR

Before you reach your limo, look for the Wash This Way Auto Detail sign. There are funny services on offer, and don't forget, tax and a BIG TIP are not included in the price.

Animation Courtyard

Quiet, unassuming Animation Courtyard doesn't provide the same thrill level as the rest of the park, but there is a real gem here, namely the opportunity to indulge in some creativity of your own.

QUESTION 1

You can still see an animator working from time to time if you check out the Ink and Paint department just beyond the exit for the *Magic of Disney Animation*, leading to the character meet-and-greet section. What does the animator wear when painting cels?

A Vinyl apron

B White gloves

C "I'm a Disney Animator" pin

D Microphone for answering questions

QUESTION 2

When the park opened, it included working studios. Now the boxy buildings just flesh out the story. What is the number of the sound stage where *Disney Junior—Live On Stage!* is showing?

Voyage of the Little Mermaid

In the Hans Christian Andersen tale, the little mermaid uses a magical flower given to her by her dowager grandmother to breathe above water and agrees to live in everlasting pain for the chance to marry her beloved. Disney's version is a bit sweeter and, in another deviation from the original, this one ends happily.

QUESTION 1

Far more than a puppets-and-live-actors show, Voyage of the Little Mermaid is a sensory experience as well. What special effects are used to make you feel as if you're in the sea?

A Blowing sand, sea spray, and bubbles

B Low oxygen levels, dangling fishhooks, and a briny smell

C Wind, rain, and laser wave effects

D Seagull cries, a waterspout, and the sound of crashing waves.

QUESTION 2

Ursula is like an obnoxious coworker who acts friendly but doesn't have your best interests at heart. What is the pet name she calls Ariel in an effort to ingratiate herself?

___

FASCINATING FACT

You're under the sea, where bubbles float up instead of down. How does Disney achieve this feat? They add helium to the bubble makers, creating a lighter-than-air final product. Of course, the bubbles do eventually come down, but watch how they hover above you for a while.

LOOK FOR

While you're waiting in the preshow area, look at all the wacky signs nailed to the walls. They give "maritime relevance" to everyday items, making folding camping stools into a place to store your wooden leg at night, or cheap yard-sale art into antique nautical paint-by-number landscapes.

The Magic of Disney Animation

Ever wonder how Disney characters come into being? *The Magic of Disney Animation* reveals the origins of Mushu, Mulan's fiery sidekick who almost had two heads, in a humorous reunion between the animated dragon and his creators.

QUESTION 1

Mushu and a host Cast Member relive the process of bringing animated characters to the big screen. When Mushu has completed his part in the show, what treat does your host present?

A An original song-and-dance number

B Beer for the adults, fruit punch for the kiddies

C A preview of a current or upcoming Disney movie

D A FASTPASS to meet Mulan.

QUESTION 2

Meeko the raccoon and Flit the hummingbird made the final animated cut, but Pocahontas was originally going to have a third companion. Which animal was it?

_____

FASCINATING FACT

Animation is the cornerstone of any Disney production, whether on film or in the theme parks. As you walk around the parks, see if you can identify which artist created the concept for each attraction. Mary Blair's characters are obvious; you'll see her style at "it's a small world." Marc Davis's characters are a blend of realism and whimsy, as seen in Pirates of the Caribbean, Haunted Mansion, and Country Bear Jamboree. Each Imagineer's distinctive style is the ultimate hidden "signature."

Disney Junior—Live on Stage!

Disney Junior—Live on Stage! is big fun for little kids. Preschooler television favorites Sophia the First, Doc McStuffins, Jake and the Neverland Pirates, and, of course, Mickey and his friends, invite youngsters to help them create a magical birthday party for Minnie Mouse, with lots of audience participation.

QUESTION 1

Every preschooler with a television knows these magic words (so ask if you have one with you!). What do you have to say to get Mickey's Clubhouse to appear at the start of the show?

A Meeska mooska Mickey Mouse!

B Open, Sesame!

C Can we find it? Yes we can!

D Wocka wocka, have no fear, make the clubhouse now appear!

Doc McStuffins makes everyone feel a whole lot better. Even her eye chart is super-kid-friendly, with an animal theme instead of letters. Which animal is at the top of the chart?

FASCINATING FACT

The first year that the Disney Junior channel was on television solidified the two-to-five age market for the House of Mouse, beating out other, more established programming. This demographic spends an average of thirty-two hours per week watching television and is considered the gateway group toward establishing brand loyalty.

LOOK FOR

You're in a room full of three- and four-year-olds, so your attention is going to be on their delightful dancing, singing, and all-around enjoyment of their favorite familiar characters. What could be more appropriate for this group than some easy-to-find hidden Mickeys? You'll find them hiding as bubbles on a few of the screens around the stage.

Mickey Avenue

Mickey Avenue used to extend from Animation Courtyard to the Studio Catering Co. near the Honey, I Shrunk The Kids Movie Set Adventure. Now it's a small section that starts at Walt Disney: One Man's Dream and ends at the archway into Pixar Place. Sometimes good things come in small packages, and the amount of Disney history in this little section of the park is pure gold.

QUESTION 1

That's one happy skull up there on the wall at the Legend of Captain Jack Sparrow. And why not? He seems to have been successful in his pirating, if his jewelry is anything to go by. Which small figures adorn the bottom of his beaded bauble?

A An angel and a devil

B Three skeletons

C A tiny gold replica of the *Black Pearl*

D The letters M, O, M

QUESTION 2

In the center of the old pirate map that is painted on the wall, you'll see a chalice. What does the banner across the front of the chalice read?

Walt Disney: One Man's Dream

From the simple dream of a place where families can come together for a happy day out, Walt Disney's genius has spread across the world, influencing movies, television, business, and even the fabric of American society. Walt Disney: One Man's Dream is a delightful historical journey from his early years to the vast empire of today. Not a bad legacy, hey?

QUESTION 1

To honor those who were instrumental in bringing his visions to life though Walt Disney Productions, Walt created an award statue featuring Mickey Mouse. What is the name he gave to this award?

A The Mickey Mouse Milestone Statue

B The Magnificent Mini-Mickey

C The Mickey's Choice Award

D The Mousecar Statue

QUESTION 2

There are so many fabulous historical gems in Walt Disney: One Man's Dream that it's like being in a Disney-geek candy store. Among them are factoids about the life and times of a certain Mr. Mouse. With that in mind, which Disney short film introduced Mickey Mouse in full Technicolor?

FASCINATING FACT

Tell someone they're "twitterpated" now and they'll probably think you mean they spend too much time on social media. Back in Walt's day, twitterpated meant you were in love. Check out the *Bambi* poster that addresses the subject of "Twitter-pation"; it's the first time this made-up word was ever used.

LOOK FOR

Where to start? Look for a recreation of Walt's office, the Abe Lincoln Audio-Animatronics from *Great Moments with Mr. Lincoln*, the "Dancing Man," models built by Walt, and the multiplane camera. How fast your heart beats as you wander through this museum of Disney history may be an indication of how much of a Disney geek you are. Don't worry if you need to rest quietly for a while when you're done; it happens to the best of us.

Pixar Place

Based on Disney-owned Pixar Studios in Emeryville, California, the area is a reconstruction of that institute of brilliance, which brought the likes of *Toy Story*, *UP*, *Cars*, and *Finding Nemo* to the world.

QUESTION I

Pixar Studios is a working production company, with all of the accompanying departments. Which Pixar department is not represented in Disney's Hollywood Studios?

A Effects

B Security

C Camera Department

D Story Department

QUESTION 2

Andy from *Toy Story* has a wicked sense of humor. A monkey from the Barrel of Monkeys is in big trouble. What is he strapped to, and what makes the situation even worse?

FASCINATING FACT

There's a lot of hard work at Pixar Studios, but a lot of play, too. Scattered around the campus are larger-than-life renditions of characters such as Luxo Jr. and WALL-E; there are foosball and Ping-Pong tables, video games, and offices that look like a shed or a cave. This kind of playful atmosphere inspires thinking that turns a cow into a tractor and a desk lamp into a beloved, child-like friend.

LOOK FOR

The Green Army Men have turned a Scrabble board into a message center. But it's not top-secret info they're spelling out. It's "You've Got a Friend in Me," a song from the movie, and *Meet the Toys*, a Golden book.

Toy Story Midway Mania!

Finally! A ride designed so that anyone can participate and feel successful. Scramble under Andy's bed and see what his toys are doing. Seems there's a midway in town, so get ready to score big.

QUESTION I

Boys can be messy, and Andy's bedroom is—let's face it—a wreck. There are toys and games everywhere. As you walk through the queue, which game boards are positioned above you?

A Chutes and Ladders and Checkers

B The Game of Life and Monopoly

C Candy Land and Scrabble

D Clue and Sorry!

QUESTION 2

Crayons, Lincoln Logs, Mr. Potato Head—they're all here in a big jumble, with little regard for each toy's intended purpose. Which characters are on the View-Master reel sticking out of a Tinker Toy when you first enter the standby queue?

FASCINATING FACT

"Blue ribbons for everyone" at this midway, but if you're really competitive and can't stand seeing others with higher scores, there *is* a trick. It's not just a matter of hitting high-point targets in the midway games. Instead, it's like a Rubik's Cube; there is a system to achieving a supersuccessful outcome. The tricks are specific enough that they could fill a fat brochure, so I'm just here to tell you that you can find tips and secrets all over the Internet, if you're so inclined. If not, just enjoy the midway and forget the mania.

LOOK FOR

As you round the corner toward the unloading area after your time on the midway, notice the Magic Slate lift-and-erase drawing pad. There's a message for you. If you were born after the 1980s, ask your parents about the satisfying sound the slate made when you lifted the plastic to erase your drawing, and watch them smile.

Streets of America

When Disney's Hollywood Studios opened, Residential Street and New York Street were part of the Backstage Studio Tour and were closed to foot traffic. Residential Street is now the location of Lights, Motors, Action! Extreme Stunt Show, but New York and the short San Francisco area remain. What's the most memorable part of this section of the park? Watch as first-time visitors look around to see if there really is a car coming.

QUESTION 1

The New York section of Streets of America has the unmistakable ring of the Big Apple, with all the noises of a major metropolis. Which business along this street is undeniably run by New Yorkers?

A Fahgettaboudit Pawn Shop

B Not fa Nuthin Jewelers

C Youse Guys Moychindice

D Mista Schleppy's Curios

QUESTION 2

In an astonishing geographical move, San Francisco is just a short stroll from New York, but the change in atmosphere is striking. What better place to land than Chinatown? If you need a lift back home, what is the number of the bus that stops just outside the Chinese Laundry?

Lights, Motors, Action! Extreme Stunt Show

Good guy, bad guys, loud cars, and explosions. What more could you want from an action movie? Even the wait time between scenes has the air of an authentic film in progress.

QUESTION 1

The show has undergone a few changes over the years, including a brief Jet Ski scene and a cameo appearance by Herbie the Love Bug. Who has taken over as Herbie's replacement?

A Benny the Cab

B RC from *Toy Story*

C Chitty-Chitty-Bang-Bang

D Lightning McQueen

QUESTION 2

Guests need an easy way to distinguish the good guy from the bad guys, and here the good guy gets to drive a shiny red car. How many different red cars are used during the show?

FASCINATING FACT

Moteurs . . . Action! Stunt Show Spectacular began in Disneyland Paris, with a setting reminiscent of Villefranche-sur-Mer on the French Riviera. Famed stunt driver Rémy Julienne coordinated the stunts for the show, having gained notoriety through his work on six James Bond movies and *The Italian Job*. He later coordinated the stunt scenes in *The Da Vinci Code*.

LOOK FOR

One of the onstage cafes, Cafe Olé, has a humorous name that seems to indicate the owner is from Spain, although its meaning is synonymous with something decidedly French. A similar pronunciation, *cafe au lait*, is the French term for "coffee with milk."

Honey, I Shrunk the Kids Movie Set Adventure

Professor Wayne Szalinski ranks right up there with some of the most irresponsible of movie fathers. Not only does he neglect to tell his children his newest invention—a shrink-ray gun—is working, he also puts the kids out with the trash and nearly eats them for breakfast. But go ahead and play in his backyard anyway and see the world from a new perspective.

QUESTION 1

When you're the size of a human, small things can easily be lost in the grass. When you're smaller than an ant, those things are pretty easy to find. Which item is not found in the Szalinski's backyard?

A A paper clip

B A Tinker Toy

C A colored Lite-Brite peg

D A bottle cap

QUESTION 2

Besides his great big sniffing nose, what other evidence do you see in the Szalinski's backyard that tells you there's a dog around?

FASCINATING FACT

While it's true that dog noses are high-tech appendages, the one here in the playground is super-high-tech. Inside that sniffing snout is a nozzle, two air ducts, an air tank, and a big speaker.

LOOK FOR

DinoLand U.S.A.'s Dig Site isn't the only place where extinct things can be found. Look for the roll of Kodacolor Gold 100 film lying in the yard. At the time the playground was built, this was premier photographic technology. Now it's pretty much gone the way of the T. rex, although a few straggling bits can occasionally be found for sale online.

Muppet*Vision 3D

In Muppet*Vision 3D Kermit and his pals appear in their first 3-D adventure, and they're making the most of it. Besides all the fun, the show is a charming tribute to the Muppets' creator, Jim Henson, who passed away exactly one year prior to his loveable characters' Disney park debut.

QUESTION 1

This is the Muppets, so you know things are going to go hilariously wrong. When Kermit asks Swedish Chef what happened to the projector, what does Swedish Chef tell him has happened?

A It's gone boom-boom.

B It's gone floomy-floomy.

C It's going bork, bork, bork.

D It's gone wocka wocka.

QUESTION 2

Poor Bean Bunny only wants love and acceptance. Instead, he gets yelled at. Who tells Bean he has ruined the film after the debacle with Miss Piggy's musical interlude?

FASCINATING FACT

When *Muppet*Vision 3D* was being imagined, it was decided the Muppets would "be aware" they were being filmed in a three-dimensional format for the first time, and they would feel awkward about it. Hence Kermit's comment about refraining from using "cheap three-D tricks."

LOOK FOR

Miss Piggy may be the star of the fountain outside *Muppet*Vision 3D*, but the real winners are the rats. Check out the two rodents in the tiny boat, fishing for coins with a horseshoe magnet.

Echo Lake

Based on the lake in Echo Park, California, Disney's Echo Lake is a relatively quiet location; it almost seems to be holding its breath. Part urban, part archeological site, things are in progress, but the glitz and glamour of Hollywood hasn't achieved a firm grip here.

QUESTION 1

There's trouble brewing above the Indiana Jones Adventure Outpost! No, wait . . . it's just a movie set. What worrisome scene has been assembled on the roof of the building?

A A rough wooden gallows

B A machine gunner's nest

C A ransacked workman's abode

D Tea for two, Nazi style

QUESTION 2

Winsor McCay, a pioneer in animation, brought the character Gertie the Dinosaur to eager vaudeville audiences, setting the stage for a certain Mr. Disney, who took the ball and ran with it. What year did the dinosaur, who appears in Disney's Hollywood Studios in concrete form, debut in the animated film, *Gertie the Dinosaur*?

Star Tours—The Adventures Continue

Every cool Star Wars planet you ever wanted to see can be explored (quickly!) on the newest offerings at Star Tours—The Adventures Continue. Don't be surprised if your tour runs into a bit of trouble, with inexperienced C-3PO at the helm and a rebel spy onboard.

QUESTION 1

Just like the *Twilight Zone* Tower of Terror's drops, you never know what you're going to get when you ride Star Tours. But there is something that stays the same: Before you launch into space, you're sure to get one of two characters demanding that

C-3PO stop the ship and release the rebel spy. Which two characters are they?

A Darth Maul and Bobba Fett

B Wicket W. Warrick and Jango Fett

C Darth Sidious and Palpatine

D Darth Vader and a Stormtrooper

QUESTION 2

As you walk through the queue toward your awaiting Starspeeder, various announcements are made over the intercom and one of them is fairly alarming. It seems the security level has been raised. What is the new security level?

FASCINATING FACT

The queue area for Star Tours is loosely based on the 1983 blockbuster hit *Star Wars Episode VI: Return of the Jedi*, around the time of the Battle of Endor. An AT-AT makes its way out of the forest, a speeder bike is parked nearby, and the Ewoks are celebrating, although you can only hear them and see their campfires after dark.

Airports of the future aren't all that different from today's airports, except for the spacecraft and weird-looking aliens. But a flight is a flight, and you're going to need some basic information. Notice the big Arrivals and Departures board shortly after you enter the queue and are making your way toward the Starspeeder 1000. If you watch for a bit, you'll notice one of the Departures destinations is Mon Calamari. Sure, it's an alien species in the Star Wars movie *Return of the Jedi*, but it really means "my squid" in French. Lunch, anyone?

Indiana Jones Epic Stunt Spectacular!

With a breathtaking start, the Indiana Jones Epic Stunt Spectacular! re-creates scenes from *Raiders of the Lost Ark* as if you were watching the actual filming, except you have an enthusiastic director to walk you through each stunt.

QUESTION 1

The opening scenes of *Raiders of the Lost Ark* are real heart-pounders, and the start of the show in Hollywood Studios lives up to that thrill factor. Which terrifying hidden danger isn't one of the impediments Indy has to avoid in his efforts to steal the golden idol?

A Falling rocks

B A big pit

C Deadly scorpions

D Axe-wielding guardian statues

QUESTION 2

Volunteers are actively recruited at the start of the show, so wave wildly if you want to be chosen. What are the four possible groups in which a volunteer might be placed?

FASCINATING FACT

In 2000, Indiana Jones Epic Stunt Spectacular! underwent its first major refurbishment since opening day, and to celebrate its return Disney invited 500 Florida residents, all with the last name of Jones, to see the "grand reopening" show. Each guest received a Jones T-shirt, a hat, and the chance to ride in a special motorcade through the park.

LOOK FOR

The ninja seems to appear out of nowhere. Watch the pile of rugs as the fight scene progresses, and you'll notice he's been hiding inside them the whole time.

The *American Idol* Experience

All the tension, all the anticipation, all the excitement of the television show, and contestants are even subjected to a cranky judge who can't resist giving them a nasty—and often undeserved—little zinger at the end of their performance. Luckily, the audience is encouraged to boo.

QUESTION 1

It's a long road from anonymity to superstardom, but the first steps might be taken in Hollywood Studios. Which one is not part of Disney's Hollywood Studios' audition experience?

A A brief interview discussing credentials

B Singing any song a cappella

C Singing a Disney-approved song with a microphone

D Singing on stage

QUESTION 2

Lucky contestants who move from the audition stage to the final cut enjoy two more phases before appearing on stage. What are they?

FASCINATING FACT

Has anyone who won a Dream Ticket actually made it to the finals on *American Idol*? Then seventeen-year-old Aaron Kelly won his Dream Ticket just four days after the *American Idol* Experience opened, and he made it to fifth place on the television show.

LOOK FOR

Recruiters! If you think you have what it takes to be a star, or if you just enjoy singing in front of a group of strangers, this is an experience you'll never forget. Look for recruiters at the front of the building in the morning or at the back of the building all day. Sometimes they even roam around the park looking for recruits. Good luck!

Fantasmic!

Mickey's imagination usually conjures up happy thoughts, but when it goes wrong . . . boy, does it go wrong! Disney's most horrifying villains want a piece of Mickey's imagination, but don't worry, it all works out happily ever after in the end.

QUESTION 1

Just as it appears Mickey is really in for it, something happens that turns the tide. What does Mickey use to help him vanquish evil?

A A sword he pulls from a stone

B Flames shooting from his fingertips

C A flamethrower hidden in his robes

D The chant "Dreams really do come true"

QUESTION 2

A freakish pachyderm dance and some curious *Pinocchio* elements kick things off, while an incredible *Peter Pan* fight scene on Captain Hook's ship takes place in Disneyland's version of Fantasmic! But those aren't the only differences between the original version in California and the transplant in Orlando. Anaheim's show is standing room only, or guests can sit on the ground. What sort of seating does the Orlando show offer?

FASCINATING FACT

The show is set on a mountain, and it doesn't look all that huge, does it? In fact, it actually hides a six-level building.

LOOK FOR

Disney animated shorts are interspersed with modern classic movies here. Just after the *Pinocchio* bubble goes up, watch for Mickey dancing with long underwear, and again during the Genie from *Aladdin* bubbles.

DISNEY'S HOLLYWOOD STUDIOS SCAVENGER HUNT

Get ready for your close-up—at least, your close-up inspection of this hunt's clues. You've been cast in the role of a super-sleuth, and now it's lights . . . camera . . . action!

1. The Pacific Electric Railway was once the largest electric railway in the world. Find a map of the railway's lines, which serviced what is now greater metropolitan Los Angeles. How many scheduled trains run daily?

2. Besides all the usual accouterments you'd expect in a 1940s movie theater's ticket booth, what surprising addition does the ticket seller at a certain legendary Hollywood theater have in her booth?

3. Rosie is doing everything she can to support the troops, and her patriotism doesn't end with the name of her restaurant. What is on the sign she has tacked up on the front of the building?

4. When Hollywood Studios opened (as Disney-MGM Studios), *The Magic of Disney Animation* was a much different experience. The walk-through tour included watching a Disney animator working on an upcoming Disney animated feature. Today there is a carving that re-creates this labor-intensive process. Where in the park can you find the carving of an animator drawing film cels featuring Donald Duck?

5. Which characters representing the afterlife are to the right of La Florida on the giant pirate map?

6. Luxo Jr., that adorable little desk lamp featured in the 1986 Pixar short film of the same name, used to make periodic appearances, but there were some wonky

goings-on with his technology so now he hangs out in noninteractive form. Where can you find him?

7. *Toy Story*'s Andy has been playing the classic American game, Battleship, and while we only see one of the two boards, things are going pretty well for this particular set-up. Even so, which two ships have been hit?

8. How many dolphins are on the fountain featured in the 1984 movie *Splash*, and how many are holding up the basin the mermaid is sitting on?

9. Most big cities have a Chinatown, and most Chinatowns have a Chinese laundry. But if you take your clothes there for cleaning, you may struggle to read the street signs. What is the only character that translates from English to Chinese on the pedestrian crossing sign in front of the Chinese laundry?

10. Hollywood's hopefuls need office space too, and at 75 cents per day or five dollars per week, it's possible they'll be able to rent an office that includes hot and cold water. There's just one problem. What is it?

CHAPTER 4

Disney's Animal Kingdom

Of all the Walt Disney World parks, Disney's Animal Kingdom is the most laid-back, and in some ways the most detailed. Here, the detail tends to be subtle, small scale, and historical. You're asked to consider how you feel about issues rather than simply experiencing the park in an auditory and visual way, and if you take the time to observe, you may find this is the most intellectually rewarding park as well.

The Tree of Life is the centerpiece and icon of Disney's Animal Kingdom, and, as park designer Joe Rohde states, it's "a celebration of our emotions about animals and their habitat." So let's start connecting to the stories the park has to tell.

QUESTION I

Though the work was done by many, the overall concept was overseen by one man, Executive Designer Joe Rohde. Because it was designed as a "whole" rather than as parts of a whole, Disney's Animal Kingdom exhibits a cohesive theme throughout the park. What is it?

A Wild by design.

B Why animals are nicer than people.

C Observe and appreciate the intrinsic value of nature.

D Conservation: Everyone has a role to play.

QUESTION 2

Name three locations on the park's property where you can still find evidence of the never-built Beastly Kingdom, which later became Camp Minnie-Mickey.

FASCINATING FACT

Although Beastly Kingdom never came into being, there *is* one element of the land's main theme that became a reality. What is it? It's the mythical beast that lives on the Forbidden Mountain, Asia's fearsome Yeti.

LOOK FOR

If Disney's Animal Kingdom is the last park you visit your photo album is probably reaching critical mass, but squeeze in these final picture-spot snaps:

- Stand near the planter in front of the right-hand ticket booth, with the **Disney's Animal Kingdom sign** over your right shoulder.
- Stand in front of the first fence you come to in front of the **Discovery Island** gardens and animal habitats, with the Tree of Life centered behind you.
- Stand next to the last lamppost on the right as you're walking toward **DINOSAUR**, then turn around so the iguanodon and the sign for the attraction are over your right shoulder.
- Stand along the walkway fence in **Asia**, to the left of the light fixture, with the temple inhabited by gibbons and siamangs to your extreme left.
- Seek out the interactive drumming spot just as you enter **Africa** from Asia. This is another chance to really ham it up! Make sure the Tree of Life is centered behind you before the picture is snapped.

Oasis

You made it through the turnstiles, you're just a short stroll away from the Tree of Life, the attractions are practically calling you by name, and it's all so exciting! But you can't see any of it yet, and that visual omission is on purpose. First, you need to decompress. Slow down. Put the hectic pace behind you and immerse yourself in a world before iStuff and instant gratification. Only then will you fully appreciate the meandering pace needed to let nature's magic catch up with you. That's the goal of the Oasis, and it performs its duty beautifully.

QUESTION 1

You know you're supposed to move through the park at a leisurely pace, but how does the Oasis help you do that?

A The sidewalks are deliberately sloped upward.

B The pathways wind around on themselves.

C Cast Members whisper the subliminal message, "Go slowly."

D Pathways are designed to be narrow so fewer people can pass through at the same time.

QUESTION 2

Nature is the focus here, without the distraction of human interaction. The ground is dry and cracked; roots poke up all around. But you still need lights along the pathway at night. What are the lampposts in the Oasis modeled after in order to keep a cohesive theme?

FASCINATING FACT

Some of the birds in the Oasis, such as the spoonbills, are given false eggs to sit on. This circumvents nature's course and prevents overpopulation by fooling the bird into thinking she has fulfilled her obligation, production-wise. With younger birds, it can clue them in to where they should lay eggs when their time comes. Clever, isn't it?

LOOK FOR

If you take the left-hand path from the Oasis, look for the bridge leading into a cave that exits into Discovery Island. It's a nice transition from nature being in command to humans making their mark.

Discovery Island

More artist colony than village, Discovery Island is a celebration—no, an explosion!—of the love of animals. The villagers have carved, sculpted, and painted animals on every available surface, sometimes grouping them according to their physical attributes or their behavioral preferences. Visitors are drawn in by the bright colors and whimsical poses, but they're also made a part of the circle of life. Notice the predator and prey motif at Flame Tree Barbecue. Now notice you're sitting on a chair representing predators, and your lunch is sitting on a table representing prey.

QUESTION 1

Animals are everywhere in Discovery Island, but only a select few are actually alive. Which attributes did Imagineers look for when choosing the wildlife living at the base of the Tree of Life?

   A Their size and color

   B Their ability to tolerate heat and humidity

   C Their beauty and playfulness

   D Their willingness to put in long hours with little pay

QUESTION 2

One of the first monuments to the world of animals is located on the left-hand side just after you cross the bridge into Discovery Island. Which two animals does this totem-style statue honor?

FASCINATING FACT

The Tree of Life doesn't just include a variety of animals; it also represents a variety of trees. Some of the bark features the long vertical strands of the cedar tree, some resembles deeply ridged oak or smooth banyan, and some is modeled after pine. The orangutan's face emerges from the split, weathered spirals of cut oak while the nearby hippo has skin that resembles the bark of a cypress. Fish scales and bird feathers have a texture reminiscent of pine, and the iguana shares the pretty, knobby characteristics of the magnolia.

LOOK FOR

See if you can find the manatee and armadillo on the Tree of Life. They were included in the cast of animals as the representatives of Florida's wildlife.

To find the manatee, enter the queue, walk to the second lamppost, and then look left. There are two manatees in front of the waterfall. The armadillo is tiny, so you have to look closely. First, find the eagle with its wings pointing upward. Look to its right, past the camel and the dolphin. The next thing you'll see is a big baboon. Now, look just above the crocodile's eye. See the armadillo's tiny face?

It's Tough to Be a Bug!

Eighty percent of life on Earth comes in bug form. Bugs do weird stuff. Weird bug stuff that freaks humans out. Such was the thinking when it came to creating a cinematic experience in the Tree of Life Repertory Theatre, but here the tables are turned. Instead of people going after bugs, the bugs come after us. Suddenly that can of Raid in your cupboard isn't quite so funny.

QUESTION 1
••

He's mean, he's angry, and he pops up in an alarming way.
What is the first reason Hopper gives for thinking humans are
bugs' biggest enemy?

A Friends don't exterminate friends

B We hate it when you spray us with stuff

C Have you ever been hit with a fly swatter? Fly swatters
hurt

D You only see us as monsters

QUESTION 2
••

When you reach the theater's lobby you can hear musical scores
for various insect-oriented shows that sound remarkably like
their well-known "human" counterparts. One of them is an
adaptation from the hit musical *The King and I*. What is the
name of the bug's version of this Broadway tune?

FASCINATING FACT

There's no doubt about it: this is one scary show, especially for
youngsters. But some of the crying you hear isn't coming from
the littlest guests; it's actually prerecorded. Listen for the baby's
cry immediately after the Termite-ator spits acid at the flea.
This serves as a transition point, putting the attention on the
intruders (you) rather than on the bugs.

LOOK FOR

Look for the "bug cave" just before you reach the section of the tree's roots where the insect actors have set up their posters. Just a little signpost along the way, giving you a sneak peek of what's to come.

DinoLand U.S.A.

Inhabited by stodgy scientists, raucous paleontology students, and the wacky extended family of Chester and Hester, owners of Dino-Rama, DinoLand U.S.A. strikes a precarious balance between superiority, playful insubordination, and cobbled-together entrepreneurialism.

QUESTION 1

In this Fossil Fun Game, it's all about gas. Which one is not among the oil companies represented in the Fossil Fueler?

A Gasdon

B Extincto

C Jurgassic

D Dinojuice

QUESTION 2

The students are digging, the scientists are inventing, and Chester and Hester are doing everything they can to get in on the action. Where in DinoLand can you see the real (but fossilized) star of their Fossil Fun Game, Whac-a-Packycephalosaur?

FASCINATING FACT

The road skirting Dino-Rama is US 498. Look for the sign with that number on it, issued by Diggs County. Why was 498 chosen? It's the opening date of Disney's Animal Kingdom (April 1998).

LOOK FOR

Disney likes to memorialize important dates, and here in Dino-Land the date it all started was 1947. That's when gas station owners Chester and Hester (or, some say, their dog) dug up a bone that set a chain reaction in motion. Scientists arrived, the Dino Institute was built, excavation has been ongoing, and Chester and Hester have been out to make a buck on it ever since. Notice the bone-casting sign over the entry to the Bone-yard. It reads: Est. 1947. You can also find this date on the notice board to the right of the Boneyard's entry.

The Boneyard

While the scientists at the Dino Research Institute are busy conducting tours back in time, the paleontology students are out dig, dig, digging. Their latest excavation is still a work in progress, and while it's hard work, there is fun to be had here, too.

QUESTION I
....

Given that you're at an archeological dig site, can you guess what the slides are meant to be?

A Mudslides

B Debris chutes

C *T. rex* femurs, split in half

D Fossilized lava tubes

QUESTION 2

There are two articulated dinosaurs in DinoLand whose bones were cast from originals found in Chicago's Field Museum of Natural History. Which two are they?

FASCINATING FACT

See that big bone casting being used as the dig site's sign? It's a casting of a *Stegosaurus* shoulder blade, but it's been modified slightly. Notice the letter *N* with an arrow? If you held the bone with north facing up, it would appear roughly the same shape as Disney's Animal Kingdom on opening day. Go ahead, compare it to your park map, and imagine most of Asia isn't there yet.

LOOK FOR

One of the students who goes by the name Animal may not be getting the highest possible grades, if his latest theory is anything to go by. Look for the note he has pasted on the *Triceratops* facts display, just to the right of the interlocking *Triceratops* skulls. His theory won't go over well, but his instructions to "party on" are likely to be even less well received.

Primeval Whirl

Chester and Hester stole the idea of time travel from the scientists at the Dino Institute, but their version is far more homespun and much more child-friendly. But beware: it packs a whirling wallop!

QUESTION I

What's a roadside attraction without its wild-mouse roller coaster? When creating Primeval Whirl, how many seconds did Chester and Hester decide it takes to go from the present to the past?

A Five

B Eight

C Twenty

D Sixty

QUESTION 2

Much of Dino-Rama is made from leftover scraps and found items. When assembling Primeval Whirl, Chester and Hester painted large plywood features to simulate your trip back in time. What is the last feature your time machine goes through at the end of the ride?

FASCINATING FACT

Before the arrival of Primeval Whirl, the area the attraction now sits on was occupied by temporary exhibits Dinosaur Jubilee and the Fossil Preparation Lab. Here, some of the bones from Dino-Sue (a replica of whom can be seen outside the DINO-SAUR attraction) were on display as they were being cleaned for their eventual reconstruction at Chicago's Field Museum of Natural History. The Field Museum placed an 8.36 million dollar bid for Sue's bones, and guess who one of the partners was in that successful bid? You got it—Walt Disney World Resort.

TriceraTop Spin

Okay, so it could rightly be called "prehistoric Dumbo," but even little dinosaurs deserve their own place in DinoLand. Besides, no self-respecting roadside carnival would be complete without its stomach-twirling hub-and-spoke ride.

QUESTION 1

Chester and Hester are a hands-on couple when it comes to Dino-Rama, but they also hired all of their extended family to keep things running smoothly. With that in mind, whose voice do you hear giving instructions as you board TriceraTop Spin?

A Chester

B Uncle Lester

C Hester

D Auntie Pester

· ·

Dino-Rama's owners are sticklers for detail, in their own way. Besides the fact you're sitting inside a baby dinosaur, how do you know you've traveled back in time as you ride TriceraTop Spin?

FASCINATING FACT

Does the shape of the attraction's center base look familiar? It's based on those spinning metal tops your grandparents played with when they were children. The handle at the top made the toy hum and spin, which was real entertainment for toddlers back in the "olden days."

LOOK FOR

To be honest, there isn't a whole lot to look for at this standard fairground ride, but you can find one little gem. If you talk to the Cast Members (briefly; after all, they are working!), you'll discover they're all relatives of Chester and Hester, hired to keep Dino-Rama running smoothly.

DINOSAUR

Why hang around a boring research institute when you can travel 65 million years back in time and return home with an iguanodon, the biggest souvenir imaginable? Sure, there's that pesky Earth-destroying asteroid to worry about, but really, what could go wrong?

QUESTION 1

What is the name Disney gave to the terrifying dinosaur menace in this attraction?

A Ingentibus pustulatae carnivora (Enormous Warty Meat-Eater)

B Formidibilis fera bula (Terrifying Savage Beast)

C Currere pro Vita Tuasaurus (Run for Your Lifeasaurus)

D Carnotaurus robustus Floridana (Stout Meat Bull from Florida)

QUESTION 2

As you journey back to the Cretaceous period, your CTX Time Rover's onboard system announces the name of each dinosaur you encounter. Which species of dinosaur is busy swallowing one of its lesser cousins?

FASCINATING FACT

The thrills are undeniable, but there is a subtle message in DINOSAUR: Nature wins over technology. Great minds at the Dino Institute created the means to travel back in time, but nature takes over once you're there. As you're careening through the Cretaceous chaos, listen for Dr. Seeker's command to "Veer left! Veer right! Veer left!" Even those simple commands go wrong. Notice which way your time rover actually moves when he shouts out orders.

LOOK FOR

When you exit the ride, take a few moments to look at how goofy you were when your ride photo was taken, then turn around and watch the television screen above your head. The institute's security cameras have discovered your mission was successful, and they're trying to deal with the aftermath. If you watch closely, you'll notice a certain Dr. Seeker is now seeking an escape route.

Finding Nemo—The Musical

From the big screen to the small stage, it's a story that never seems to get old no matter how many times it's told. And it's told a lot. Nemo's friends and family just can't seem to keep track of him. But this version is among the most creative; it's a musical worthy of a place next to its African cousin, *The Lion King*, under the bright lights of Broadway.

QUESTION 1

When Nemo says he wants to go home and calls for his dad, the fish in the tank tell him his dad is back at the pet shop. Nemo is confused by the term, so they each tell him where they're from. Which place is not mentioned?

A Bob's Fish Mart

B Fish-o-Rama

C PetSmart

D eBay

QUESTION 2

What is the excuse the sharks give Marlin and Dory during their "intervention," when Bruce—who, they say, isn't really so bad—has suddenly turned savage after Dory gets a nosebleed?

FASCINATING FACT

Clownfish have a hierarchy within their community. Marlin and Coral would have been the dominant fish in their anemone, and the only ones to raise a family. All clownfish are born male but are able to switch gender when they mature. While they're abundant and aggressive in the wild, they're rather fragile in captivity. Darla wouldn't have to shake the bag to shorten Nemo's life; just living in a tank would, sadly, make his days numbered.

LOOK FOR

The show is so beautiful that it would be a shame to spend it looking for some small detail. Relax and enjoy the musical, and look for an interesting "historical marker" outside instead. See the round courtyard area at the front of the building? When Disney's Animal Kingdom opened, this circular section marked the end of this side of the park. There was no Asia area or Dino-Rama; there was just DinoLand U.S.A. and the open-air, tented Theater in the Wild. Even the walkway that now leads to the front door of the theater wasn't there yet. Weird to think of it that way, isn't it?

Asia

Many adventurers dream of climbing Mount Everest or undertaking a challenging white-water-rafting excursion, and local entrepreneurs are only too happy to help those dreams come true. But the villagers of Serka Zong and Anandapur are not so sure. They're aware of the dangers faced by these big tourist draws, when respect for nature is ignored. But go ahead and make that dream of yours come true . . . at your peril!

QUESTION 1

There are many symbols of protection around Anandapur, including slashes of red paint on businesses, shrines, and statues. But which two items, hung up by homeowners, are edible?

A Garlic and onions

B Garlic and chili peppers

C Basil and oregano

D Sage and fennel

QUESTION 2

Chakranadi River is under threat, as you discover during your river-rafting tour, and all of Anandapur is up in arms about it. As you walk around town, you'll see fliers reminding locals that the destruction must be stopped. What is the name of the logging company responsible for local deforestation?

FASCINATING FACT

See the fabric squares waving in the wind above your head, along with banners and strips of material hanging from trees and bells throughout Asia? Those are prayer flags, and although they are not symbolic of actual prayers here in Disney's Animal Kingdom, Imagineers did choose to include one tradition attached to them: The flags are allowed to decay on their own and are never taken down.

LOOK FOR

Sometimes you have to get creative with your problem-solving, and Anandapur has done just that. With a nod toward "thinking outside the box," look for the two Coke bottles being used as glass insulators on the light pole just before the queue to Kali River Rapids.

Expedition Everest: Legend of the Forbidden Mountain

At one time the village of Serka Zong was thriving, mainly on the back of the tea plantation that provided the area's main export. Then, things began to go wrong. Superstition about the Yeti kicked into high gear. There were holdouts, of course, including the owners of Yak & Yeti Restaurant in nearby Anandapur, and a couple of entrepreneurs who knew an easy buck when they saw one. Now, those old tea trains have a bright future. Or do they?

QUESTION 1

When designing the Forbidden Mountain, Imagineers wanted a sharp, craggy, scary look to the rockwork. To help achieve that, they used traditional sculpting tools and a common household item, which they pressed into the wet cement. What kitchen item was used to make random, spiky impressions over the façade of a giant mountain range?

A The back of a slotted spoon

B A heavy-duty sponge

C Dishtowels

D Big strips of crunched-up aluminum foil

QUESTION 2

Before the Forbidden Mountain, there was another snowy attraction that was originally intended to include a ferocious beast. While the Yeti never arrived at that attraction, a cousin of his found his way there in 1978, and the experience became an even bigger hit. In 2006, the Yeti made his debut here at Disney's Animal Kingdom. Which attraction at another Disney park was an inspiration for Expedition Everest?

Kali River Rapids

There is an element of fun to floating along Kali River Rapids, but the message of the destruction wrought by deforestation is serious. And while the splashdown finale is wonderful on a hot day, it's meant to symbolize the land giving away and chaos ensuing when nature no longer exists to hold it all together.

QUESTION I

You're almost at the end of your journey, and so far you've only gotten a few splashes on the back of your shorts. But you're not done yet. Which Asian animals disguised as water cannons should you watch out for after you make the final pass under a bridge before unloading?

A Camels

B Yaks

C Elephants

D Sea squirts

QUESTION 2

In an effort to generate income through eco-friendly tourism rather than slash-and-burn logging, which Anandapur resident opened the Kali Rapids Expeditions?

FASCINATING FACT

Go ahead and call that wild-haired masked character at the far-right corner of the Tiger Temple "Bucky." He won't mind if you laugh at his overbite, since he's got bigger things on his mind. His real name is Sida Karya, and he often acts as a priestlike figure, the presenter of offerings to the gods, in traditional Balinese storytelling. In the intricate Topeng Pajegan dance, Sida Karya's role comes at the end of the performance. After he presents his offerings, he throws coins to the children in the audience. He then captures a child and symbolically makes his final offering, ultimately releasing the child with a special gift for his or her participation.

Maharajah Jungle Trek

Maharajah Jungle Trek and its African counterpart, Pangani Forest Exploration Trail, are wonderful examples of why Disney's Animal Kingdom is a zoo that's not a zoo. It has all of the animals, but none of the cages, and it also has a beautiful, inspiring story.

QUESTION I

There are hints everywhere that a long time ago something terrible happened here. Now, nature has taken control of what was once the domain of humans. What was the Maharajah Jungle Trek before it opened to the public as a peaceful walking tour?

A A zoo created for the amusement of the royal family

B The hunting and leisure grounds of the maharajahs

C The royal palace of the maharajahs

D A private club for the wealthy of Anandapur

QUESTION 2

Some buildings have to do double duty when you live in a remote village, and the community center shares its space with the local bat population. But that doesn't put a damper on the villagers' fun. What's on their calendar for every Saturday this month?

FASCINATING FACT

When you reach the deer enclosure, just after the tiger area, look at the tree on the right-hand side, inside the enclosure. See those wind chimes? They're there for two reasons: First, they're a fun toy for the deer to bat around, and second, they encourage the deer's natural desire to spar with their antlers.

LOOK FOR

Sometimes you have to make use of common items to solve everyday problems. Look at the ceiling as you pass through the first small building leading to the Maharajah Jungle Trek. See those newspapers laid out over the beams? Just as American pioneers knew the value of newspaper for insulating their homes, so too have Anandapur's residents discovered a creative use for this cheap, plentiful resource.

Flights of Wonder

Anandapur's maharajahs once kept exotic birds and animals here, but now Flights of Wonder belongs to the citizens, who have made it a focal point for their research and conservation efforts.

QUESTION I

As the birds' natural behaviors are showcased, an annoying tour guide, Guano Joe, butts in and disrupts what is shaping up to be an educational exhibition. His excitable mental state turns the documentary into a comedy. What phobia does he say he suffers from?

A FOB (fear of birds)

B SF (stage fright)

C FONAF (Fear of nests and feathers)

D ATS (angry tourist syndrome)

QUESTION 2

The stars of Flights of Wonder exhibit natural adaptations, but they are also proficient at learned behaviors. During the show, trainers use cues—a word, a touch, a hand motion—to elicit a response from their feathered friends. What is the cue used by the trainer to get an answer out of a mathematically inclined African parrot?

FASCINATING FACT

Why is this location called the Caravan Stage? *Caravan* has a couple of meanings that apply here: "excursion" and "group traveling together." You're on an excursion along the Silk Road, traveling with a large and diverse group. Some who come to the caravan's resting place are selling their goods and some are buying (see all those rugs hanging around?), but the main attraction is the research focused on exotic birdlife. While the story was much clearer in its original incarnation, the theater retains its name and some small semblance of its meaning.

LOOK FOR

After the hawk flies overhead, watch for the rats scurrying along the far-right building's ledge as Guano Joe talks about the rat problem Anandapur used to have but (he believes) doesn't have any more.

Rafiki's Planet Watch

Entertainment is the hallmark of any Disney park, but a bit of overt education never hurt anyone, and that's what you'll find at Rafiki's Planet Watch. Still, in best Disney style, it's not textbooky or preachy; instead it's hands-on, with plenty of Cast Member interaction. The experience starts with a journey from a train depot based on the thatch-roofed stations found in East Africa and ends with a world of information about how you can make a difference.

QUESTION 1

Let's be honest: there isn't a whole lot to see on your train journey from Rafiki's Planet Watch back to Harambe, but the trip from Harambe to Planet Watch is worthwhile for the view of a backstage area of the park. In the section you pass, animals from Kilimanjaro Safaris, such as antelope, lions, warthogs, and rhinos, spend the night in safe enclosures. Which safari residents are the only ones that do not return to a nighttime enclosure?

A Elephants

B Giraffes

C Alligators

D Ostrich

QUESTION 2

With all the working labs and surgeries at Conservation Station, you're bound to come across some pretty funky stuff. After all, animals can't tell us much about what's going on inside them, so researchers and veterinarians have to use other means to figure it out. One poster in particular takes a rather comical approach to the subject of testing animal hormones. What is the funny subtitle that sums up the two everyday bodily functions used to determine hormone levels?

FASCINATING FACT

How do you know when the Wildlife Express (or any train, for that matter) is approaching a crossing? The conductor blows the whistle in two long and then two short blasts. Want to know an easy way to remember it? Imagine the whistle saying, "Here . . . comes . . . .the train!" You'll never hear it the same way again, will you?

LOOK FOR

Cast Members give small-animal demonstrations, several times daily. Some of them are creepy-crawly (the small animals, not the Cast Members), so if you're squeamish, check out the animal's Nutrition Center food prep area or the Affection Section instead. If there is a surgical procedure going on, it's a must-see experience (unless you're squeamish, in which case, heed the previous advice).

Africa

Situated on the edge of the savanna, Harambe is a modern town coming to terms with its technologically advancing society and the opportunities for ecotourism. At one time, poaching was a problem and the locals are still on the lookout so they can take action against this destructive practice. Since the 2012 re-imagining of Kilimanjaro Safaris' story, the main issues have become observing and conserving.

QUESTION 1

Enterprising business owners in Harambe are not afraid to do whatever it takes to bring in the tourist dollars. Which dining location in Harambe has painted the bold claim, "Best Food in East Africa" on their front wall?

A Tusker House Restaurant

B Dawa Bar

C Tamu Tamu Refreshments

D Hotel Burudika

QUESTION 2

If you make a significant mental stretch, you could argue that the business indicated on the front of the restroom building and the actual function of the building both have to do with water, but what does the painted sign on the front proclaim is the building's intended use?

FASCINATING FACT

Take a look at the writing on the far-left column of the restrooms next to Tamu Tamu Refreshments. In Swahili, it reads: *Hakuna ruhusa ya kufunga mifugo mbele ya ukuta huu.* The English translation is "No permission to install livestock at the front of this wall." Sorry, you'll have to take your cows elsewhere.

LOOK FOR

Harambe was once occupied by the British, and there are some remnants of foreign rule still in evidence, including a British postal box, just to the left of the restrooms. Disney Cast Members are supposed to collect the mail in this African outpost every day except Saturday and Sunday. But wait a minute. When you've finished looking at the postal pickup details, take a look at the mail slot. Seems they're taking more than just the weekend off!

Pangani Forest Exploration Trail

It's a peaceful walking trail and an animal adventure, but, most important, it's a research project. As part of "the story," this is where Dr. K. Kalunda and his student researchers observe animals in their natural habitats. As part of Disney's Animal Kingdom's dedication to conservation, the park provides information useful to the Gorilla Species Survival Plan.

QUESTION I

Which animals are not seen along the Pangani Forest Exploration Trails?

A Hippos

B Naked mole rats

C Ostrich

D Günther's dik-dik

QUESTION 2

Dr. Kalunda specializes in researching animals in the wild, but he is also concerned about animals needing special care. Because of this, he has set up a place for colobus monkeys that require extra attention. What is the name of the center he has created?

FASCINATING FACT

Gorillas are smart. In fact, they are so smart that they need lots of mental stimulation to stay happy and healthy. With this in mind, they are often given interesting toys to play with, such as blankets, pots and pans, balls, and even those small plastic rocking horses toddlers enjoy.

LOOK FOR

One of the researchers, Rebeccah Davis, has been researching hyenas over on the escarpment, taking extensive notes, photographing group members, making vocalization tapes, and recording social interactions. You can find the results of her work at the scientific research center. However, you won't find live hyenas along Pangani Forest Exploration Trail or anywhere in the park. They are considered too vicious to be kept safely here at Disney's Animal Kingdom.

Kilimanjaro Safaris

Mud wallows, rocks warmed by the sunshine, pools to swim in, and trees to scratch against are all "behavioral opportunities," but they're really there to allow the Kilimanjaro Safaris' animals to get out there and be themselves. That dedication to realistic environments—and the chance that a rhino or a giraffe might walk up to the open-air vehicle you're touring in—is what makes Kilimanjaro Safaris so special.

QUESTION 1

What does the answering machine found in the office along the queue claim that Kilimanjaro Safaris does when it comes to the safari experiences they offer?

A We keep on truckin'!

B We put on hip waders and stir up the crocodiles for the best photos ever!

C We promise hippos and elephants but aren't so sure about rhinos.

D We go wild!

QUESTION 2

Every business needs a license, and Kilimanjaro Safaris' small trader's license, found in the office along the queue, allows them legally to offer which two things?

Festival of the Lion King

Based on the hit movie *The Lion King*, the *Festival of the Lion King* was the first in-park show to include a Cirque du Soleil–meets–Broadway style of entertainment. The original story has a new chapter here, with a traveling troupe joining Simba, Timon, and Pumbaa as they celebrate the Lion King.

QUESTION I
....

Four entertainers whose Swahili names hold special meaning lead the traveling troupe performing today. Which name is not included in the translations they give you?

A Masculinity and Strength

B The Gift

C Princess

D Prince

QUESTION 2

Timon isn't afraid to join right in when the Tumble Monkeys take center stage, but his fellow jungle residents aren't so quick to leave their stations. What is the reason Pumbaa gives for not joining Timon on stage?

FASCINATING FACT

How did the quintessential story of wildlife surviving and thriving on the African savanna end up in a campground in New York's Adirondacks at Camp Minnie-Mickey? It all goes back to that pesky Beastly Kingdom. When plans fell through for the area (meaning, funding was not approved), something had to be put in the open space intended for the never-built land. Cue the Character Experiences meet-n-greets! But Camp Minnie-Mickey was still lackluster and bare. Cue the incomprehensible Pocahontas and Her Forest Friends, a simple show added to flesh out the area, and the more heavily-invested-in *Festival of the Lion King*, one of Disney's most innovative shows, that still pulls 'em in fifteen years later. Happily, the show's move from Camp Minnie-Mickey to its rightful place in Africa only adds to the magic.

LOOK FOR

Okay, this is just goofy, but if you're able to see Pumbaa's backside from where you're sitting, watch his tail. Bob to one side, bob to the other side, give a little wiggle . . . it certainly has a life of its own! Animals . . . they're so comical, aren't they?

DISNEY'S ANIMAL KINGDOM SCAVENGER HUNT

Like the great explorers throughout history, you've got a lot of ground to cover in search of this park's treasures. You won't need binoculars or a backpack for your adventure, but a little animal instinct wouldn't hurt.

1. Shortly after you enter the roots of the Tree of Life, you'll see a cave with a waterfall next to it. Notice the salmon leaping upstream. Which other animal is, appropriately, nearby?

2. The bugs are hungry for great entertainment; that's why they have their own theater inside the Tree of Life. Apparently, that's not all that whets their appetites. What, specifically, have they done to the posters advertising the latest shows?

3. When Chester and Hester's Dino-Rama first opened, the couple only charged fifty cents for parking. Now that they're popular, they've raised the price. Find the billboard that reflects this price hike. How much are they charging now?

4. Your quest is to seek out large fossilized bones that don't belong to a dinosaur. Where are they and what animal are they from?

5. Every business in Anandapur has been issued a license and a permit. What is the number on the permit given to Gupta's Gear by the Ministry of Economic Development, and in what year was it issued?

6. Look for a framed Notice of Life-Guard Qualifications granted to the proprietor of a certain ecotour by the Anandapur Ministry of Public Safety. There is a notice

next to it whose content should make river rafters nervous. Who issued this notice?

7. Prayer ribbons are common in Asia, but so are prayer tablets. Find the prayer tablet with a carving of two skeletons.

8. Jorodi Masks & Beads company offers exceptional East African art, and they'll even ship it to you, if desired. What is the phone number you can reach them on?

9. Mombasa Marketplace is undergoing reconstruction. Who is doing the restoration?

10. Conservation-minded researchers keep copious notes, sometimes about things that may be ever-so-slightly distasteful. One student, studying hippos, has drawn a twofold conclusion: Grass + Hippos = Dung. What does the second conclusion indicate?

CHAPTER 5

Bonus Scavenger Hunts

Guests of all ages can enjoy the scavenger hunts for Magic Kingdom, Epcot, Disney's Hollywood Studios, and Disney's Animal Kingdom, but here you'll find hunts designed for two very special groups: children and longtime Disney fans.

The Kid's Scavenger Hunt is an easy, exciting adventure created with youngsters in mind. And because it's for children (though parents and older siblings may want to join in too), the location each clue leads to will be right out in the open. Kids will enjoy the thrill of the hunt, and the "I can do it" pride that comes with success.

The Die-Hard Scavenger Hunt will prove demanding even for Disney fans who have seen it all, done it all, and have the T-shirt to prove it. But that's half the fun! Clues are vague, so you really have to know your stuff, but if you're ready to accept the challenge this die-hard hunt will certainly prove rewarding.

Kids (and Kids-at-Heart) Scavenger Hunt

This isn't school, it's Walt Disney World! This means that there's no need for you to write anything down for your scavenger hunt; simply have someone take a picture of you with each item as you find it, and check it off the list. Then, when you get home, print out all the photos. If you saved your birthday money, you could even buy a scrapbook and make your own souvenir with the pictures you took.

As you go from park to park, watch out for two things in each land, pavilion, or area of that park. Then, get snapping! Bear in mind, you don't have to ride any attractions to participate. Everything is outside the rides, so don't worry about long lines. Now, let's go hunting for . . .

Magic Kingdom

Main Street, U.S.A.

☐ A Dapper Dan (*hint:* they're real people and they sing)

☐ A horse's head hitching post

Fantasyland

☐ A gargoyle or a centaur

☐ La Fontaine de Cendrillon (*hint:* it's French for "Cinderella's fountain")

Liberty Square

☐ A colonial stockade (Go on; put your head in it!)

- ☐ Ghostly horseshoe tracks (Your picture will come out best if you crouch down and point.)

Frontierland

- ☐ Br'er Bear and Br'er Fox looking for Br'er Rabbit (How do they not see him?)

- ☐ An erupting geyser

Adventureland

- ☐ Ice cream (not really; I just thought you might need a refreshment break)

- ☐ A Tiki god

- ☐ A giant rock that looks like a skull (*hint*: thar be pirates nearby!)

Tomorrowland

- ☐ An intergalactic telephone

- ☐ Something with Stitch in it

Storybook Circus

- ☐ Peanuts (Do that crouching and pointing maneuver again.)

- ☐ Anything squirty! (With you in it, if today is hot.)

Epcot

The Seas with Nemo & Friends

- ☐ Find Nemo! (*hint*: look for his "lucky" fin to be sure you have the right clownfish)

☐ A shark whose mouth you can stick your hand into

The Land

☐ The sticky-uppy strata outlined in red tiles and black tiles on the mural that represents layers of Earth (You know "sticky-uppy" isn't a real geological term, right?)

☐ Timon and Pumbaa bashing a sign into the ground

Imagination

☐ Figment, the little purple dragon (Any Figment will do—be creative!)

☐ A picture of Figment, dressed up as a "little stinker"

Universe of Energy

☐ A mini landscaped area (*hint*: it looks like a Jurassic jungle that you can stand in front of and pretend something inside is terrorizing you)

☐ If you've used a lot of energy and it's hot, find something along the path leading from Electric Umbrella to Universe of Energy that you can stand under to cool off.

Mission: SPACE

☐ The big red spot on Saturn

☐ A moon landing that is closest to the date you were born

Test Track

☐ Two giant Coke bottles that would explode from all the spinning if they were real

☐ A gigantic version of the *T* that joins the words *Test* and *Track* (*hint*: you walk under it)

Mexico

☐ A parrot that looks as if he's alive (Stick around for a few minutes and maybe he'll say something.)

☐ A great big stone wheel with a guy sticking his tongue out at you

Norway

☐ A troll, but not just any troll. The biggest troll in the pavilion (rub his belly for good luck)

☐ A Viking who looks like he's about to slay something

China

☐ A Foo Dog (Mom Foo has her foot on a baby; Dad Foo has his foot on a ball)

☐ A tomb warrior who looks like he just heard a really funny joke

Germany

☐ A gecko sitting on a rooftop, stalking a car, or acting like Godzilla in the train display to the right of the pavilion

☐ A pickle ornament (It isn't a true German tradition, but it's kind of fun to see pickles on a Christmas tree.)

Italy

☐ Something you would use to get around if you lived in Venice (*hint*: they have canals instead of streets)

☐ A wooden skull crusher . . . I mean, grape press

The American Adventure

☐ A painting that shows schoolchildren having a lesson in a way most kids wish their teachers would allow

☐ A free souvenir (You can get one by volunteering for the Spirit of America Fife and Drum Corp band and become a Son or Daughter of Liberty.)

Japan

☐ A warrior on horseback

☐ A goldfish the size of a wiener dog

Morocco

☐ Someone (could even be you!) wearing a fez (*hint*: it's a hat)

☐ A carpet you wish the Genie would cast a spell on so it could fly

France

☐ A friendly gargoyle

☐ A place where you can pretend to sell books, postcards, and priceless paintings

United Kingdom

☐ A fountain with a fish that looks like a dolphin

☐ A red mailbox (because red phone booths are too obvious)

Canada

☐ Something on a totem pole that looks like a fox with an upside-down person below him

☐ The entrance to a mine (but if you sit on the big chain, you'll get rust on your bottom . . . so don't do that)

Disney's Hollywood Studios

Hollywood Boulevard

☐ A film director made of bronze who thinks *you* should be a star!

☐ Your feet in the footprints of Roger Rabbit (If you're not a fan of Roger Rabbit, choose a character you like.)

Sunset Boulevard

☐ A yellow City Cab (Pretend you're telling the driver you don't have enough cash for the fare.)

☐ A stop-and-go signal with railroad tracks running past it and a fire hydrant nearby

Animation Courtyard

☐ Your favorite "under the sea" fish

☐ A metal filmstrip featuring Mickey Mouse

Pixar Place

☐ One of Andy's drawings

☐ A cookie jar with Woody on it

Streets of America

☐ An umbrella attached to a lamppost (Go on . . . pull on the handle!)

☐ A snowman . . . yes, there really is a snowman in Florida.

Echo Lake

☐ Something giant, made of metal, with huge legs and a menacing look

☐ You doing exactly what the sign next to the rope going into the well tells you not to do

Disney's Animal Kingdom

Oasis

☐ Noisy red, blue, and yellow parrots perched on a rope or a branch (If it's too hot or too cold for them to be out, or it's past their bedtime, point at their empty perch and make a sad face.)

☐ A secret passageway through the rocks

Discovery Island

☐ Your favorite wild animal (It could be on the Tree of Life, in a sculpture or a painting . . . anywhere!)

☐ A Disney Wildlife Conservation pin

DinoLand U.S.A.

☐ A *Triceratops* skull big enough to sit on

☐ A naughty dinosaur who took a bite out of the sign he's holding (*hint*: he's really big)

Asia

☐ A crumbling statue with great big clawed feet (Go ahead and sit on the bench between the feet)

☐ A gorilla's handprint cast in metal (Is your hand almost as big as his?)

Rafiki's Planet Watch

☐ Rafiki (find your favorite one)

☐ An animal handler with an animal you'd like to meet (bonus points if you ask him or her a question)

Africa

☐ An advertisement for Kinga Hot Air Balloon Trips

☐ Someplace where you can do your best African drummer impression; go wild!

Die-Hard Scavenger Hunt

With special thanks to Marcus D'Amelio, Interactive Event Designer–WDWCelebrations Core Team, who created this Die-Hard Scavenger Hunt. Marcus says, "Over the past several years it has been my privilege as the Interactive Event Designer for WDWCelebrations to create various activities for our event participants. Over the course of celebrating the anniversaries of the founding of each park, I created a series of challenging scavenger hunts, meant to challenge our players to seek the details that the creators of these magical places placed for us to notice, and by doing so, learn more about the world in front of them and the world outside these magical gates."

Now let's see how much you *really* know about Disney! There are few hints here, so part of the challenge is in figuring out where to find each item. Regardless of the level of success you have, you can still claim serious bragging rights just for trying.

Magic Kingdom

1. The Main Street windows are famous among Disney fans. Who is listed on the window as the owner of Chimney Sweep Pest Control?
2. Who presented President Jefferson with a fossilized Mastodon tooth?
3. What company provides Tomorrowland's videophone service?
4. What is the name of the hopscotch variant found in Adventureland?

Epcot

1. What is the ID number of Agent Havoc?
2. What is today's theme at the Imagination Institute?
3. What is the name of the first unmanned moon landing?
4. In what year was the picture of Stonehenge sketched in the explorer's journal?

Disney's Hollywood Studios

1. The Echo Lake Apartments seem like quite a nice place to live. In which apartment do Empero and Zovich reside?
2. How many miles are there on the "Scenic" drive?
3. What item is shown in quotes as part of "Plan B" at the Green Army Men Command Post?
4. In the victory garden, how is the scarecrow dressed?

Disney's Animal Kingdom

1. Which animal is *not* depicted in the mural in the largest dining room at the back of Pizzafari: a snail, a spider, a stork, a chipmunk, or an iguana?
2. What is the motto of Stego-Soda?
3. What is the name of the rich merchant who turned his home into the Yak & Yeti Hotel?
4. What is the Kiswahili name for the baobab tree near the entrance of the safari?

If you enjoy this challenging scavenger hunt, be sure to check out WDWCelebrations at *www.wdwcelebrations.com*. Cofounder Adam Roth and his team put on fantastic events, and the proceeds go to worthy charities, like our personal favorite, Give Kids the World (*www.gktw.com*). We hope to see you at an upcoming event!

Afterword

And . . . . pencils down! Feel like an expert now? If you knew many of the answers, you can rightly claim to be a die-hard Disney fan. If you didn't, don't worry. You're well on your way to expert status and have all the tools you need to amaze your friends with this vast array of trivial and not-so-trivial Walt Disney World tidbits. But most of all, you can explore the parks in a new way, with a new appreciation for the depth of the experience that awaits you. When you pay your next visit to Walt Disney World, open your eyes wide and be amazed by what you see!

Note!

Want to share your pictures? Flag them on our Facebook page, hiddenmagicofwdw. Include your name (or your Facebook name), the month and year you visited Walt Disney World, and a one- or two-sentence comment about your trip. Keep in mind that by supplying us with access to your picture, you are granting permission for that picture to appear on our Facebook page and you understand you will not receive compensation of any kind for its use. Family-friendly pictures only!

Trivia Answer Keys

Chapter 1: Magic Kingdom

MAGIC KINGDOM:

1. D
2. Remember the Magic

MAIN STREET, U.S.A.

1. B
2. Artist and concept designer, Harper Goff. Goff was also instrumental in creating the storyboard art for classics such as the former 20,0000 Leagues Under the Sea attraction.

WALT DISNEY WORLD RAILROAD

1. C
2. Roger E. Broggie

FANTASYLAND

1. B

2. Cinderella's Golden Carrousel, Dumbo the Flying Elephant, "it's a small world," Mad Tea Party, Peter Pan's Flight

PRINCE CHARMING REGAL CARROUSEL

1. C

2. It's a chariot featuring a golden eagle and Lady Liberty holding an olive branch.

THE MANY ADVENTURES OF WINNIE THE POOH

1. D

2. A fly swatter . . . with honey on one corner

MAD TEA PARTY

1. A

2. Charles Lutwidge Dodgson

ENCHANTED TALES WITH BELLE

1. A

2. "You've got big drawers to fill."

UNDER THE SEA ~ JOURNEY OF THE LITTLE MERMAID

1. C

2. She's acting as a merry-go-round for baby seahorses.

SEVEN DWARFS MINE TRAIN

1. B

2. The cars swing and sway individually. Suspended coasters have done this, but standard track coasters have not.

MICKEY'S PHILHARMAGIC

1. A
2. "Auto-magic" doors

PETER PAN'S FLIGHT

1. D
2. You can see his shadow pass by on the nursery wall.

"IT'S A SMALL WORLD"

1. A
2. *The Three Caballeros*

LIBERTY SQUARE

1. D
2. The Province Bell, the State House Bell, the Bell of Independence, the Bell of Revolution, the Herald of Freedom

THE HALL OF PRESIDENTS

1. C
2. Valerie Edwards

HAUNTED MANSION

1. C
2. The one-eyed cat

LIBERTY SQUARE RIVERBOAT

1. B

2. The river doesn't take kindly to uninvited guests.

FRONTIERLAND

1. B

2. Only Country Bear Jamboree and Frontierland Shootin' Arcade are original. The original Frontierland Train Station was demolished and replaced by a new version in 1992.

COUNTRY BEAR JAMBOREE

1. D

2. Al Bertino. Al was a show writer for Disneyland's Country Bear Jamboree. He worked on such classics as the Pirates of the Caribbean and the Haunted Mansion.

SPLASH MOUNTAIN

1. D

2. A beehive

BIG THUNDER MOUNTAIN RAILROAD

1. A

2. $1.40

TOM SAWYER ISLAND

1. C

2. A trading post

ADVENTURELAND

1. B
2. A. Smith, better known as Arabella Smith, from the 2011 movie, *Pirates of the Caribbean: On Stranger Tides*

PIRATES OF THE CARIBBEAN

1. B
2. *Wicked Wench*

JUNGLE CRUISE

1. A
2. *Walt Disney's True-Life Adventures*

WALT DISNEY'S ENCHANTED TIKI ROOM

1. D
2. "It's out the door you go!"

THE MAGIC CARPETS OF ALADDIN

1. C
2. A scarab beetle

SWISS FAMILY TREEHOUSE

1. C
2. A barrel and half of a giant clamshell

TOMORROWLAND

1. B
2. *Just Imagine* (1930) and *Things to Come* (1936)

MONSTERS, INC. LAUGH FLOOR

1. D

2. SLUG

BUZZ LIGHTYEAR'S SPACE RANGER SPIN

1. D

2. 1.5 megavolts

WALT DISNEY'S CAROUSEL OF PROGRESS

1. C

2. Jim

TOMORROWLAND TRANSIT AUTHORITY

1. B

2. Mr. Johnson in the control tower

ASTRO ORBITER

1. A

2. Astro Jets, Tomorrowland Jets, and Rocket Jets

SPACE MOUNTAIN

1. D

2. Generating a Bright New Tomorrow

STITCH'S GREAT ESCAPE!

1. B

2. A DNA scan

TOMORROWLAND SPEEDWAY

1. D

2. Strike the car ahead of you

STORYBOOK CIRCUS

1. D

2. Fair Weather Place

DUMBO THE FLYING ELEPHANT

1. B

2. Believe and Soar!

THE BARNSTORMER

1. D

2. *Aquamania*

CASEY JR. SPLASH 'N' SOAK STATION

1. A

2. He crossed using a hose.

Chapter 2: Epcot

EPCOT

1. D

2. There were not enough pavilion sponsorships for World Showcase to justify opening it as a separate entity.

SPACESHIP EARTH

1. B

2. This, our Spaceship Earth

THE SEAS WITH NEMO & FRIENDS

1. B

2. Dawn to Dusk

THE LAND

1. D

2. Spring and summer

LIVING WITH THE LAND

1. B

2. Nine; there are three of each

SOARIN'

1. B

2. Another hang glider appears as you're flying over Yosemite National Park.

THE CIRCLE OF LIFE: AN ENVIRONMENTAL FABLE

1. C

2. Hakuna Matata All-Electric Lakeside Disco Village

JOURNEY INTO IMAGINATION WITH FIGMENT

1. A

2. Imagination

CAPTAIN EO

1. D

2. His robot transforms and dislodges its leg to create a guitar.

INNOVENTIONS EAST AND WEST

1. B

2. Agent Quench battles Scorchers (dehydration), Agent Dynamo battles Sappers (distractions), and Agent Fuel battles Blocker Bots (junk food).

UNIVERSE OF ENERGY

1. A

2. Lava from volcanic eruptions

ELLEN'S ENERGY ADVENTURE

1. C

2. The air-conditioning and Jacuzzi period

MISSION: SPACE

1. D

2. *Ranger 4*, which landed on April 23, 1962.

MISSION: SPACE (THE RIDE)

1. A

2. The North Polar Cap

TEST TRACK PRESENTED BY CHEVROLET

1. D

2. The mirror to your right shows a graphic of airflow streaming above your car.

MEXICO

1. C

2. *Papelidos*, which translates to "little papers"

GRAN FIESTA TOUR STARRING THE THREE CABALLEROS

1. A

2. Sunglasses, a snorkel, and a diving mask

NORWAY

1. D

2. A dragon's head and a sea serpent's body

MAELSTROM

1. B; two in the mural in the loading area and three along your journey

2. Milestones in Norwegian Exploration

CHINA

1. C

2. d.c. ying

REFLECTIONS OF CHINA

1. A
2. Water

GERMANY

1. A
2. A crown and a castle turret

ITALY

1. C
2. Grapes, apples, pears, and lemons

THE AMERICAN ADVENTURE

1. B
2. Rosie the Riveter

JAPAN

1. C
2. The yin and yang symbol

MOROCCO

1. B
2. A glass roof is hidden above the bamboo roof.

FRANCE

1. D
2. Over the Arcade breezeway, next to the Plume et Pallete

IMPRESSIONS DE FRANCE

1. A
2. He has made a hat out of grape leaves and is wearing it.

UNITED KINGDOM

1. A
2. Christmas Day and Boxing Day

CANADA

1. C
2. 13. Three large and four small poles outside and six inside the far-right section of Northwest Mercantile

O CANADA!

1. C
2. The *Bluenose* schooner

ILLUMINATIONS: REFLECTIONS OF EARTH

1. D
2. 34

Chapter 3: Disney's Hollywood Studios

DISNEY'S HOLLYWOOD STUDIOS

1. A
2. The Darkroom, which is shaped like a camera

HOLLYWOOD BOULEVARD

1. A
2. Pluto has Pluto's Toy Palace.

THE GREAT MOVIE RIDE

1. C
2. Putty Nose

SUNSET BOULEVARD

1. B
2. Sunset, Gower Echo Park, and Melrose Avenue

BEAUTY AND THE BEAST—LIVE ON STAGE

1. C
2. Angela Lansbury, Mrs. Potts from the movie

THE TWILIGHT ZONE TOWER OF TERROR

1. B
2. Mahjong

ROCK 'N' ROLLER COASTER STARRING AEROSMITH

1. D. What else could it be, since it's connected to a car?
2. The highway is congested and you're advised to take an alternate route.

ANIMATION COURTYARD

1. B
2. Sound Stage 5

VOYAGE OF THE LITTLE MERMAID

1. C
2. Angelfish

THE MAGIC OF DISNEY ANIMATION

1. C
2. A turkey

DISNEY JUNIOR—LIVE ON STAGE!

1. A
2. A whale

MICKEY AVENUE

1. B
2. Aqua de Vida

WALT DISNEY: ONE MAN'S DREAM

1. D (pronounce it like "Oscar" rather than "mouse car")
2. The 1935 short, *The Band Concert*

PIXAR PLACE

1. B

2. He's strapped to The Big One—a bottle rocket fire work—and a nearby monkey is holding a match.

TOY STORY MIDWAY MANIA!

1. A

2. Characters from the movie *Peter Pan*

STREETS OF AMERICA

1. C

2. #46

LIGHTS, MOTORS, ACTION! EXTREME STUNT SHOW

1. D

2. Three

HONEY, I SHRUNK THE KIDS MOVIE SET ADVENTURE

1. D

2. A giant pawprint

*MUPPET*VISION 3D*

1. B

2. Sam Eagle

ECHO LAKE

1. B

2. 1914

STAR TOURS—THE ADVENTURES CONTINUE

1. D

2. Level 5

INDIANA JONES EPIC STUNT SPECTACULAR!

1. C

2. Screamers, Laughers, Posers, and Junior Directors

THE *AMERICAN IDOL* EXPERIENCE

1. A

2. Time with a vocal coach and a session in hair and makeup

FANTASMIC!

1. A

2. Orlando's show has metal bench seating

Chapter 4: Disney's Animal Kingdom

DISNEY'S ANIMAL KINGDOM

1. C
2. The sign over the ticket booths featuring a dragon's head, on the backs of directional signage inside the park, and the Unicorn section of the parking lot

OASIS

1. A
2. Bamboo plants

DISCOVERY ISLAND

1. C
2. Rhinoceros and birds

IT'S TOUGH TO BE A BUG!

1. A
2. "Hello Dung Lovers," a parody of "Hello Young Lovers"

DINOLAND U.S.A.

1. D
2. In the Boneyard, to the left of the entry, just past the second slide

THE BONEYARD

1. B

2. Sue, the *T. rex* outside the DINOSAUR attraction, and the brachiosaurus on the Olden Gate Bridge near the Boneyard

PRIMEVAL WHIRL

1. A

2. An interlocking wooden model of a dinosaur skull

TRICERATOP SPIN

1. C

2. There are comets "flying" above you.

DINOSAUR

1. D

2. *Alioramus*

FINDING NEMO—THE MUSICAL

1. C

2. He never knew his dad.

ASIA

1. B

2. Tetak Logging Company

EXPEDITION EVEREST: LEGEND OF THE FORBIDDEN MOUNTAIN

1. D

2. The Matterhorn at California's Disneyland Park

KALI RIVER RAPIDS

1. C
2. Manisha Gurung. You can hear her welcoming you and describing the tours as you enter the Kali Rapids Expeditions office.

MAHARAJAH JUNGLE TREK

1. B
2. Feast Day! Find the calendar on the left-hand wall after you enter the building.

FLIGHTS OF WONDER

1. A
2. The trainer ends each question with the word *three*.

RAFIKI'S PLANET WATCH

1. C
2. All in a drop; All in a plop

AFRICA

1. A
2. The Harambe Port Authority

PANGANI FOREST EXPLORATION TRAIL

1. C
2. Endangered Animal Rehabilitation Center

KILIMANJARO SAFARIS

1. D

2. Photo-safari Tours for Multiple Parties and Special Itinerary Tours

FESTIVAL OF THE LION KING

1. D

2. His legs are too tiny for him to get down off his float.

Scavenger Hunt Answer Keys

Magic Kingdom Scavenger Hunt

1. They scored one run in the third inning and one run in the fifth inning. Find the scoreboard behind the bleachers in Casey's Corner.
2. Nine arrows were shot, one hit the bull's-eye. Find the arrows in Gaston's Tavern holding up the menu signs.
3. You should get eighty-four. Each gargoyle has two tusks, two horns, and ten toenails. Find them on the bridge leading to Be Our Guest Restaurant.
4. It mentions the *Fanny S. Perley*. Go up the steps on the right after you enter Columbia Harbour House, then look for the sign on the wall on the right-hand side.
5. "And don't ever spit in front of women and children." Find it in the doorway to Pecos Bill Tall Tale Cafe.

6. Six deer shed their antlers. Find them above Frontier-land Shootin' Arcade.

7. The Swiss Family reached the tree on July 17, 1805. Find their story in the landscaping to the right of the entry to the queue.

8. This pirate is in a crow's-nest above the sign for Pirates of the Caribbean, looking at the stage where Jack Sparrow does his shows.

9. Little Blue Alien Is Big Trouble. Find it in the newspaper stand in Tomorrowland.

10. "The biggest little star in the galaxy" is Sonny Eclipse, lounge lizard at Cosmic Ray's Starlight Cafe. His suit is purple.

Epcot Scavenger Hunt

1. He is the Manager of Everything Else. Find his titles on his office door as you walk through the queue in Journey Into Imagination with Figment.

2. It would be six months.

3. It's in the Bijutsu-kan Gallery, in a case along the back wall on the right-hand side.

4. This plaque is the first one you see as you make your way up the ramp to the Mission: SPACE FASTPASS machines. It reads: *To all who follow their dreams 'to infinity and beyond.'*

5. You'll find these figures in the wood carving around the door that leads into Stave Church Gallery in Norway.

6. You'll find the skull and antlers in Norway, on the side of the Kringla Bakeri og Cafe near the restrooms.

7. You'll find the three-clawed dragon on the light fixture attached to the wall in the dining area to the right of the cash registers.

8. The map is inside the open green bouquiniste box on the wall in front of the France pavilion.

9. The proverb is inside Fez House to the left of the wall fountain.

10. E. Wood won the cow trophy; Henry Thomas had the best chicken. Both trophy cups can be found on shelves inside the Crown & Crest in the United Kingdom pavilion.

Disney's Hollywood Studios Scavenger Hunt

1. Twenty-seven hundred trains run every day. Find the map on the back of the small building on the corner of Hollywood Boulevard and Sunset Boulevard that displays attraction wait times.

2. She has a little sink. Find it at Legends of Hollywood on Sunset Boulevard.

3. Rosie's sign says, "Stay True to the Red White and Blue." Find it on Rosie's All-American Cafe in the Sunset Ranch Market on Sunset Boulevard.

4. Look at the arches to the right and left of the main archway leading into Animation courtyard. The animator is on the left side of each arch.

5. A skeleton and an angel represent the afterlife. Find them on the wall of the building housing the Legend of Captain Jack Sparrow.

6. Luxo Jr. sits on top of the Pixar Place street sign to the left of the Pixar Studios arch.

7. The five-peg destroyer and the two-peg patrol boat/ destroyer have both been hit. Find this board upside down on the ceiling of the gift shop across from *Toy Story* Midway Mania!

8. There are four dolphins, but none of them are holding up the basin. Find the fountain near the restrooms by *Honey, I Shrunk the Kids* Movie Set Adventure.

9. The "walking man" character is the same in both languages.

10. There is another sign next to it that reads: No Actors. Find both signs above the Hollywood & Vine restaurant in Echo Lake.

Disney's Animal Kingdom Scavenger Hunt

1. You will find a bear, just off to the right

2. They've eaten small holes in them. Find them on the left side of the queue as you head toward the It's Tough to be a Bug! theater.

3. A large billboard to the right of Primeval Whirl, at the back of Dino-Rama, shows they are now charging $2 for parking.

4. These large fossilized bones are in the Dig Site and they're the bones of a woolly mammoth.

5. The number on the permit is 8640 and it was issued on May 29, 1933. Find it on the front of Gupta's Gear, to the right of the four-paneled doors.

6. Anandapur Wildlife and Forestry Authority issued this notice. You'll find it on the far wall in the Kali Rapids Expeditions office.

7. This tablet is the eighth one from the right, along the left-hand side of the central wall as you face Serka Zong Bazaar.

8. The phone number is 287-952-8795 and you'll find it listed on paper signs on the buildings around Harambe. Some are hard to read, so keep looking if the number on the first one you find is illegible.

9. Mjafari Architectural Restoration Company is doing the reconstruction. Find their green permit sign on the wall to the right of the front entry in Mombasa Marketplace.

10. The student's note says, Dung in Water = Tilapia and Fish-Hunting Birds. Find the notes to the right of the underwater hippo viewing area in Africa.

Solutions to Die-Hard Scavenger Hunt

MAGIC KINGDOM

1. It is listed as Walsh's Chimney Sweep Pest Control. Find the window to the left of The Emporium Gallery, on the second floor of The Emporium.

2. William Clark of the Lewis and Clark Expedition pre-sented the tooth. Find the tooth in the first glass case on the right-hand side as you enter the lobby.

3. Galactic Communications Network provides the ser-vice. Find the name in the Metrophone booth under Astro Orbiter.

4. Island Hop is the name of the game. Find it on the left side of the floor as you walk into the shop.

EPCOT

1. The identification number is 125485 (HAVOC). You'll find this number on Agent Havoc's ID in the top right corner of the screen at the start of the driving challenge game, as your agent status is being checked.
2. "How to Capture your Imagination." Find it on a sign on the wall in the ride vehicle boarding area.
3. *Luna 2* was the first unmanned moon landing. Find it on the moon mockup on the left-hand side of the courtyard at the entry to Mission: SPACE.
4. The picture was drawn in 1908. Find it in an open book on the left-hand side of the bookshelf behind the Kid-Cot table in the U.K. pavillion, just before the Character Greeting area.

DISNEY'S HOLLYWOOD STUDIOS

1. They live in Apartment 204. Find the mailboxes at Echo Lake Apartments, between Hollywood & Vine restaurant and the Tune-In Lounge.
2. It is forty-nine miles long. Find this number on a street sign on the left side of the road, just before the big San Francisco backdrop.
3. "Top Secret Message Decoder." Find it taped to the back window of the small building on the right-hand side, immediately after you pass under the Pixar Place sign.
4. He's dressed as a pilot. Find him in Rosie's victory garden, to the right of Catalina Eddie's in Sunset Ranch Market.

DISNEY'S ANIMAL KINGDOM

1. The chipmunk is not in the mural. Find the snail in the grass below the tiger, the spider above the red fire-alarm box, the stork in the tall grass below the fox, and the iguana below the lion.
2. The motto is "Dying of Thirst?" Find the neon Stego-Soda sign in the Hip Joint inside Restaurantosaurus in DinoLand U.S.A.
3. Arjun is the name of the merchant. Find his story on the back of the menu in Yak & Yeti Restaurant in Asia.
4. It's Mzee Mbuyu. Find the name on a sign on the baobab tree, just before you reach the FASTPASS machines.

Index

About the Author

Susan Veness is a travel writer, researcher, and itinerary planner specializing in Florida, Disney, and the theme parks. A former online travel agent, she became principal research assistant for the U.K.'s bestselling *Brit's Guide* travel series in 2002. She also writes for a wide variety of newspapers, magazines, and other media. She has been visiting Walt Disney World since it opened in 1971; with a home just minutes from The Mouse, she continues to tour the parks on a regular basis.